ALLEN COUNTY PUBLIC LIBRARY

ACPL ITEM S0-CBG-958

DISCARDED

3 1833 03238 9147

VGM Oppor

331.
Banning, Kent.
Opportunities in purchasing
careers

OPPORTUNITIES IN **PURCHASING CAREERS**

Kent Banning

Foreword by
R. Jerry Baker, C.P.M.
Executive Vice-President
National Association of Purchasing Management

VGM Career Horizons
NTC/Contemporary Publishing Company

Library of Congress Cataloging-in-Publication Data

Banning, Kent B.
    Opportunities in purchasing careers / Kent B. Banning : foreword
by R. Jerry Baker.
        p.   cm.   — (VGM opportunities series)
    ISBN 0-8442-2327-1. — ISBN 0-8442-2329-8 (pbk.)
    I. Purchasing—Vocational guidance.   2. Purchasing agents.
I. Title.   II. Series.
HF5437.B35   1997
658.7'2'02379—dc21   97-29044
                                                            CIP

Allen County Public Library
900 Webster Street
PO Box 2270
Fort Wayne, IN 46801-2270

Cover Photo Credits:
Top left, copyright © Tom McCarthy/Photo Network; top right, courtesy
Radiological Society of North America, copyright © Oscar & Associates, Inc.,
Chicago; bottom left, courtesy Softbank Comdex, Inc.; bottom right, courtesy of
International Business Machines Corporation. Unauthorized use not permitted.

Published by VGM Career Horizons
An imprint of NTC/Contemporary Publishing Company
4255 West Touhy Avenue, Lincolnwood (Chicago), Illinois 60646-1975 U.S.A.
Copyright © 1998 by NTC/Contemporary Publishing Company
All rights reserved. No part of this book may be reproduced, stored in a retrieval
system, or transmitted in any form or by any means, electronic, mechanical,
photocopying, recording, or otherwise, without the prior permission of
NTC/Contemporary Publishing Company.
Manufactured in the United States of America
International Standard Book Number: 0-8442-2327-1 (cloth);
                                    0-8442-2329-8 (paper)

15 14 13 12 11 10 9 8 7 6 5 4 3 2 1

CONTENTS

ABOUT THE AUTHOR

Kent Banning is a writer and former director of education for the Arizona Multihousing Association where he was the administrator of property management certification programs and taught courses in personnel, business management, and purchasing. This position, however, represented his second career after retiring from the University of Connecticut where he worked in purchasing administration for twenty-two years.

Mr. Banning graduated from the University of Connecticut with a major in Industrial Psychology and a minor in Business Administration. Upon graduation, he accepted a position as business advisor to private sector organizations affiliated with the university. In 1958, he developed a centralized purchasing system that eventually included warehousing, distribution, and a product testing lab.

Although under his direction the organization grew to include centralized accounting, data processing, accounts payables and receivables, personnel, maintenance, training, and working capital investment, he continued his involvement with purchasing in both the private and public sectors. He was a member of the Purchasing Standards Committee for the State of Connecticut and on numerous other committees for purchasing and specifications. He taught courses in institutional purchasing for the university's adult education center. He also developed and operated a centralized food and supply purchasing system for local hospitals.

After his second retirement, Mr. Banning became a freelance writer and has now authored seven books and over seventy magazine articles on subjects relating to small business management, purchasing, property management, franchising, and career change.

FOREWORD

Since the first edition of *Opportunities in Purchasing Careers,* the role, responsibilities, and influence of purchasers have been greatly expanded.

Once, the focus of purchasers was on the transaction and on satisfying the internal customer. Today, purchasers continually examine the supply chain process to ensure the organization's competitive position and that external customers' needs are met. The concepts of continuous improvement, strategic alliances, and supplier management have been added to the purchaser's responsibility.

With the increased influence and contribution to the organization's success, purchasers find new and challenging career opportunities. The restructuring of today's business organization and global competitive pressures bring new opportunities for the development and implementation of innovative strategies and processes. While restructuring and reinventing the corporation occurs in private industries, governments are initiating reform efforts to reduce internal processing and more closely follow commercial practices. There are enormous opportunities for the creative individual who is willing to accept the challenges of providing purchasing and supply management leadership to a variety of organizations, both public and private, large or small.

If you are a person who looks for opportunities, challenges, and a rewarding career, such an opportunity awaits you in the purchasing and supply management field.

> R. Jerry Baker, C.P.M.
> Executive Vice-President
> National Association of Purchasing Management

ACKNOWLEDGMENTS

I would like to thank the following individuals and organizations for their help in making this book possible.

R. Jerry Baker, Karen Peterson, and the National Association of Purchasing Managers for their willingness to share their wealth of information and knowledge.

Dave Cameron, Alex Marshall, and the Purchasing Managers Association of Canada for their valuable help.

The Purchasing, Transportation, and Operations Department of Arizona State University for their educational information.

Dave Hall and the Arizona Purchasing Managers Association for helping me locate experts in the various fields.

Christopher Daniels, Mark Held, Ray Gunther, Jay Selby, James Chapman, Jr., Steve Pottinger, Robert Lutz, Sandy Spain, Steven Dye, and John Mihelich for sharing their success stories.

INTRODUCTION

For those of you investigating a new career direction, the profession of purchasing may not be as familiar as sales, marketing, or finance. Yet, few professions are as old as purchasing or as critical to the success of any business activity. For any business or organization to exist, materials and services must be bought or purchased—or to use an earlier term, bartered for.

The art of bartering is as old as the human race. The earliest recorded history describes how people bartered, exchanging one thing of value for another. Bartering was practiced by the merchants in the street markets and the traders. To barter successfully, these businesspeople needed a sense of the value of things exchanged and a skill in the art of offer and counteroffer, demand and counterdemand, known then and now as haggling. In fact, the art of bartering is still practiced in every country today.

The emergence of money as a medium of exchange simplified the transfer of goods and services considerably. Theoretically, money was a thing of constant value and, therefore, eliminated the guesswork on at least one side of the transaction. People bought an item for money—they bartered one thing for another. Bartering, however, seems to imply the necessity of a greater skill. The word inspires a mental image of two men squatting in a village square engaged in skillful negotiations over how many sheep a camel is worth.

Despite the fact that it has been practiced for centuries, purchasing has been recognized as a highly skilled profession only during the past five decades. Educational institutions developed majors and concentrations in purchasing at the graduate and doctoral levels in the 1980s, again giving an indication of the recent acknowledgment of the importance of the purchasing function. In business and government, the responsibilities of the purchasing department have evolved from simply buying products and services to being completely involved with these products and services from the time a need is identified to the delivery of the finished product to the consumer.

To the person investigating this field as a possible career direction, two aspects of purchasing are attractive. First, there are a variety of opportunities. Every product and service that exists must be bought and sold—everything from paper clips to space shuttles. Second, opportunities in purchasing extend to the ranks of upper management—in most cases, the vice-president level—thus providing a career path with high income potential. It is important to note, however, that each industry has its own requirements in terms of systems knowledge, product knowledge, and personality traits. Your investigation should go beyond the elements of purchasing or procurement as a profession. You must also investigate the part that purchasing plays in each industry. Only then will you find the career track that is the best for you.

CHAPTER 1

PURCHASING IN MODERN BUSINESS

The purchasing function in modern business is still in a mode of dramatic transition—very understandable if you consider the changes in general business structures and strategies over the past two decades. There are numerous factors causing these changes, including but not limited to increased global competition, technological advances, downsizing, and the flattening of the top management structures. The impact of these shifts in the business environment has resulted in a repositioning of the purchasing function with greater emphasis on long-term business strategy and less emphasis on the more mechanical tasks of price comparisons and order placement. The modern purchasing department is more often involved in locating new sources, marketing, and research and development, resulting in a need for purchasing professionals with a greater understanding of the overall operations and goals of a company.

Those interested in a career in purchasing will find that it is necessary to anticipate the current trends and direction of the purchasing function. Since you can forecast the future only if you understand the past, the events leading up to the present state of the profession are examined below.

THE HISTORY OF PURCHASING

The principal objective of any business or government organization has always been the timely production of products or services at a competitive price or cost. Although the objective has not changed significantly since the Industrial Revolution, the method of obtaining that objective has changed dramatically, and few business functions have changed as much as the field of purchasing. During the late 1800s and the early 1900s, obtaining the necessary materials and services for the production of manufactured goods was considered to be a relatively simple part of the total process. Each department bought its own materials or services; for example, the front office bought its own office supplies, the production department bought its raw materials, and the maintenance department bought its own parts. Usually a clerk in each department was responsible for the purchasing function and there was little or no attention paid to procedures or methods. The result was often disaster from the standpoint of profitability or cost control—overstocks, understocks, no inventory control, production completely halted because of a lack of material and services, low-quality or incorrect components, out-of-control delivery schedules—all problems that contributed to the demise of many businesses active during that period.

The late 1930s witnessed a surge in war-related products for European markets, and American industry began to gear up to meet that need. Mass production techniques, only recently developed, were introduced in the manufacture of arms, machinery, vehicles, and other instruments of war as both America and its European allies prepared for the conflict that was certain to come.

Mass production systems, however, required a far more sophisticated method of procuring and scheduling raw materials, component parts, and contract services than existed at that point. Meeting production quotas in a timely manner became a matter of survival instead of simply earning profits, and management began to realize that planning, ordering, scheduling, and stocking critically needed material and services was not just a clerical function. In fact, it was during this wartime period that the purchasing function began to emerge as a true profession and a significant part of overall management.

During the past six decades, the purchasing function has evolved from a disorganized pattern of buying to meet immediate needs to a highly sophisticated method of controlling the flow of materials and services from the design of a product to the delivery of the product to the customer. From one viewpoint, the term *purchasing* is becoming obsolete. To most people, purchasing means buying, and the scope of the responsibilities of the modern purchasing department goes far beyond the ordering or buying of products and services. Today, the purchasing department is involved in preliminary product or service needs assessment, the design of specifications for raw materials and subcontracted components, cooperation with sales to ensure that the product meets customer specifications, identification of potential sources of supply, bid or contract preparation and evaluation, negotiations, transportation requirements, scheduling, receiving, inspection, expediting, and vendor performance critique. Considering the current dimensions of the purchasing function, it is not surprising that the term *materials management* is increasingly being used to describe these responsibilities.

To help you understand the variety and diverse opportunities in the purchasing field, we will explore in greater detail some of the operations of a typical purchasing or materials management department. You will see immediately that the amount of interfacing and support both given to and received from other departments is more than is involved with most other functions. Keep in mind that 50 to 60 percent of every dollar received by the company or organization is expended for the purchase of goods and services.

Since purchasing controls, or at least influences, the cost of these goods and services, it also controls or influences profitability. Since the marketplace controls the price of the finished goods or services, the purchasing department's influence over both basic raw material costs and the efficient and timely delivery of these raw materials to the production line is critical to the success of the company.

THE FUNCTIONS OF THE
PURCHASING DEPARTMENT

Preliminary Needs Assessment and Planning

Whenever a company or organization considers a new product, a major change in production methods, or an acquisition of a new business or product line, an idea begins the slow evolution into a concept. The test as to whether the concept is feasible and potentially profitable has two components. First, is there a market? Second, what is needed in terms of materials, skills, and space to turn the concept into a profitable reality? The first component is obviously the responsibility of the market analysts. The second, however, may be the responsibility of the chief executive officer (CEO), the strategic planning department, or, in some cases, a planning committee. Regardless of the person or group responsible for developing the plan, the purchasing department is an essential part of the process. Critical to the success of any plan is the cost. The purchasing department is the logical choice to furnish not only cost estimates but availability and market forecasts. Planning also usually involves projections of production and delivery dates, information that depends upon data that only purchasing can provide. Changes in product or production processes invariably involve subcontracting of components or services. Again, the purchasing department is best equipped to provide cost and availability data.

Perhaps the greatest contribution that purchasing can make in the development of new products is the establishment of quality standards. During the past decade, the consumer has become considerably more quality conscious, and the American manufacturer has had to meet quality standards that have been set by the competition. Quality must start at the planning stage, and the purchasing department obviously has a major role in establishing raw material and component standards.

Specifications Development

A specification is a very detailed and precise description of a product or a service to be purchased. It is the basic tool of the purchasing process because it serves as the communication link between the buyer and the seller, ensuring that there is a complete and common understanding as to the nature of the product or service being bought or sold. In government purchasing, the specification is the basic element of the bidding process. Product or service specifications are published or publicly distributed to ensure that all interested vendors have an equal opportunity to quote prices for the item.

Specifications are not limited to just the physical description of the item to be purchased. Other conditions of purchase, such as packing method, transportation mode, delivery schedules, and count or payment schedules, may be part of the specification.

Specifications are usually the result of a joint effort by several departments. Engineering, the using department such as production or maintenance, quality control, and the legal department may all be involved in developing specifications for a product or service.

At this point, an ongoing controversial subject comes to the surface. There are varying opinions concerning the amount of technical knowledge that the purchasing department needs to buy effectively. The answer probably depends on the items being purchased and the way the buying organization or company is

structured. In some organizations, the degree or amount of cooperation between the purchasing, technical, and using departments
is so effective, the purchasing department can rely on the other
departments to provide the necessary knowledge and information.
In other situations, however, the specifications writers and the
buyers must rely upon their own technical knowledge.

It is not at all unusual for spec writers and buyers to transfer
from technical or using departments into purchasing because of
their previously gained knowledge and experience concerning certain products and services. Many buyers of chemicals, electronics,
and other highly technical products have educational and work
backgrounds involving those products.

Customer Specification Compliance

Very often, sales of products or services, particularly sales of
component parts, are based on specifications furnished by the customer, who will specify certain types of raw materials or chemical
processes. Again, the need for cooperation between sales, production, and purchasing is easily recognized.

Identification of Potential Sources of Supply

Many purchasing departments are, in reality, libraries of product and service information. Setting up and maintaining vendor
and product files, catalogs, and records is time consuming but
necessary if the department is to have potential sources of supply
at their fingertips. Regardless of the completeness of the files,
vendor salespeople are still indispensable. Their input about availability, market conditions, product changes, and supply projections are essential to effective purchasing procedures.

Purchasing departments are second only to sales as far as outside business contacts are concerned. Consequently, they have an

important impact upon the overall image of the company or organization. Contacts may be made within the company's offices or at the vendor's offices since, in many cases, an evaluation of the vendor's facilities is part of the standard vendor selection process.

Often the needs of the organization are broken down into product and service categories. Each category will have an assigned buyer or buyers, and it will be that person's responsibility to maintain current sources of supply. Again, the amount of knowledge that the buyer must have about his or her product or service category will differ from company to company.

Bid, Quote, or Contract Preparation

Once a need for a particular product or service is identified and the specifications prepared, the purchasing department is ready to begin contacting potential suppliers. The methods by which the contact is made are numerous. In some cases it is merely a matter of picking up a phone and calling several approved vendors for prices and possible delivery dates—an example of open-market buying. Some of the other methods of contact may include:

- Formal bidding. A system used extensively by governmental agencies and state, federal, and municipal governments and institutions. The formal bidding system consists of an invitation-to-bid document outlining the conditions of the purchase, item specifications, required delivery schedules, and other requirements and limitations. Often the bids are kept sealed and opened at a public meeting.
- Request for quotation. Similar to the formal bid in that invitations to quote are mailed to interested vendors, but the quotes received are not open to the public and there is usually no requirement that the item be purchased from the lowest bidder.

- Indexed pricing. Used extensively with items that will be repeatedly purchased. The price is indexed to some commonly accepted trade or industry standard.
- Negotiated contracts. Much of today's purchasing is accomplished through the use of negotiated contracts. A vendor or vendors are selected on the basis of some criteria other than those items under negotiation. Details of the transaction are then worked out through give and take on the part of both parties.

These techniques are only a few of the many variations used in the purchasing process. This stage of the purchasing procedure, however, is the opening gambit in the actual buying of the product or service.

Negotiations

Practically every purchase of a product or service involves some type of negotiation. Even when the price is already established, conditions surrounding the purchase still have to be negotiated. For example, delivery schedules have to be coordinated with optimum inventory levels, and terms of payment have to be agreed upon. Special conditions may be imposed upon delivery systems or storage. It is not unusual for negotiations to be involved before the final specifications and conditions are prepared, especially in formal bidding situations.

Numerous departments are often involved in the final negotiating stage. Finance is concerned with cash flow and payment schedules, production is concerned with packaging and assembly, inventory control is concerned about delivery schedules, and quality control or engineering is concerned about inspection. Consequently, the purchasing department often acts as a coordinator between the various departments and the vendors.

In one sense of the word, purchasing is negotiating. In every step of the process, from design to delivery, the purchasing department is involved, reconciling opposing points of view, separating desire from reality, and attempting to arbitrate disputes. Since in many instances purchasing is the focal point surrounded by many departments, each with their own needs and priorities, it is no small wonder that negotiating skills are called upon every hour of the day.

Transportation

Practically every purchase of raw materials or products involves some type of transportation. The combination of technological advance and deregulation now offers the traffic manager a wide range of choices. Since rates are now controlled by the marketplace instead of by government regulation, the choice of transportation can have a significant impact upon the ultimate cost of the product.

The traffic manager often must make critical decisions involving cost versus timing factors. Saving money on freight rates is not necessarily cost efficient if the product arrives late and causes the production line to be shut down.

Often, the request for quotation or bid will include quotes for transportation alternatives, particularly if the buyer is responsible for freight costs. In these instances, usually the traffic manager is also responsible for checking freight billings to ensure accuracy.

Ordering

Once all of the preliminary investigations of the various vendors are completed, the buyer is ready to make a final decision as to what supplier or suppliers to use. These decisions are based on numerous factors: quality, service, reliability, capacity, price, and any other technical or delivery requirement that is considered critical to the successful procurement of the right product at the right time. Often it is also the buyer's responsibility to clear all purchase orders and contracts through the legal department to ensure that all contract conditions, stipulations, and limitations are enforceable. Since this process can be a lengthy one, most companies try to use as many standardized contracts and purchase orders as possible.

At this point, complete and effective communications between the buyer and the seller are critical. Each party to the transaction must thoroughly understand the terms and conditions of the contract or purchase order. It is not unusual to have numerous meetings between various departments of both the buying and the selling companies at this stage of the purchasing process.

Although every step of the procurement of products and services requires attention to detail, the need to be completely accurate is critical at the time of commitment. A purchase order or a contract is a binding agreement to buy and to pay for—an agreement that may commit the company to thousands or millions of dollars—and any inaccuracy or mistake can be exceedingly expensive. Unfortunately, the courts pay very little attention to unintentional mistakes when interpreting a written purchase order or a contract.

An important part of the ordering process is the scheduling of deliveries. Warehousing of raw materials and component parts represents a major cost factor, and, therefore, it is necessary to balance or weigh the savings realized from volume purchasing against the cost of storage and handling. Many companies reduce warehousing or storage and handling costs by arranging deliveries to correspond with production needs. Obviously this approach requires close cooperation with the production department in order to develop a precise delivery schedule.

It is at this point that the function known as expediting becomes critical. The expediter continuously monitors deliveries and materials handling to ensure that all product and service needs are on time and coordinated. Effective expediting requires, whenever possible, a knowledge of a vendor's past delivery performance record and, in many cases, on-site product inspection at the vendor's facilities.

In smaller businesses, expediting is often a buyer's responsibility. That is, the person actually placing the order is responsible for the timely delivery of the product or service.

Because the expediter has contact with so many of the functions of a purchasing department, the position is often used as a training ground for beginners in purchasing.

Receiving and Inspection

Although many companies separate the purchasing and the receiving function principally to reduce the possibility of collusion, the separation presents some enormous difficulties. The receiving department is the logical point of inspection. The purpose of inspection is to determine whether the product meets all the standards imposed by the specifications, a determination best made by the purchasing department. In some situations involving standard grades, for example, if the receiving department is not as knowledgeable as the buyers about the characteristics of various grades, then the whole purchasing system breaks down. Perhaps the most graphic example of ineffective inspections occurs in the hotel and restaurant industry. Because the receiving department does not have the necessary expertise in determining the grades, types, and varieties of foods, very often incorrect merchandise is accepted.

Obviously the receiving and inspection function is a critical part of the entire materials management process. If an incorrect or

3 1833 03238 914 /

defective product is interjected into the production process, the result can be catastrophic in terms of both money and reputation.

Quality Control

Usually the quality control department is a separate entity reporting directly to top management. Purchasing, however, is a major player in determining and maintaining quality standards. The adage "the whole is only as good as the sum of the parts" emphasizes the need for total cooperation between quality control and purchasing. At a time when the quality of American-made products is being questioned by consumers, the purchasing department's role in establishing and maintaining quality standards is both basic and critical. No matter how efficient production may be, it cannot make a quality product from inferior materials and components.

In actuality, high quality can only be maintained by a constant commitment from every department involved in the production process—from initial product design and engineering through delivery. The purchasing department's contribution crosses all departmental lines, however, simply because its commitment must not be limited to the actual raw materials and components used in production but must also include the tools, equipment, and contractual services used by all.

Vendor Performance Critique

Any company intending to stay in business in today's competitive environment must continuously review and analyze every aspect of its operations. One of the purchasing department's most important reviews is the critique of vendor performance. Simply stated, the critique asks, "Did the vendor deliver the right product, at the right quality and quantity, at the right time and place, at the right price?"

The vendor critique is another example of the purchasing department's responsibility to interface with many other departments. It is necessary to obtain feedback from the using departments in terms of product quality, delivery, and overall performance. The vendor critique, particularly in larger companies, is usually highly structured because of the large number of buyers and departments involved.

The vendor critique is becoming increasingly important because of a marked trend in purchasing philosophy. In the past, buyers would maintain several sources of supply for almost every item for purposes of pricing and supply. At this point, the trend is headed in the direction of increased negotiated buying from fewer vendors, marking the development of a partnership between the buyer and the seller rather than an adversarial relationship. Since, in one sense, the buyer is putting all his or her eggs in one basket, every effort must be made to ensure that the basket is the right one. The primary use of the vendor critique is to evaluate the overall performance of a vendor and to assess the risk of future negotiated contracts.

THE IMPORTANCE OF PURCHASING

At this point, it should be obvious that the purchasing department's contribution to the stability and the profitability of the company is critical, a fact that most top management teams are fully aware of. Consequently, members of the purchasing staff are usually involved in most major decisions made at the top level. Their input regarding the cost and availability of products and services is the foundation of most production plans, and obviously the timely flow of materials used in production has a definite impact on cash flow. An overview of most company operations will show that there are few functions that do not require involvement with the purchasing staff at one point or another.

Considering the wide range of circumstances requiring an interface with other departments, it is easy to understand why someone considering purchasing as a career should have a thorough knowledge of business operations in general. The ability to understand the dependency of one department upon another is essential to the effective coordination of the many services the purchasing department provides.

CHAPTER 2

TYPES OF PURCHASING POSITIONS

The variety of positions available within any one company depends upon several factors. Obviously size is a major determinant as to the scope of the purchasing function. Smaller organizations may have only one to three positions with clerical support while larger corporations or government agencies have several subdepartments and hundreds of employees. The number of products will also determine the complexity and the size of the purchasing department, since the diversity of the products will affect the number of technical specialties required.

The complexity of the product manufactured will also affect purchasing requirements. For example, an aircraft manufacturer whose single product requires hundreds of thousands of parts needs a larger complement of buyers than an auto manufacturer who makes thousands of cars in a day but uses fewer parts.

Another factor that is extremely important in determining the scope and the size of the purchasing department at any one location is the purchasing philosophy of the company. Many firms believe strongly in centralizing the purchasing function while many others feel just as strongly that decentralizing that function is the most efficient way to procure materials and services. Still another segment of the firm will develop the specifications and the master contracts in a centralized department but will allow the branches to determine their own requirements and do the actual ordering and receiving.

15

The size and complexity of the purchasing department depends upon the position of the company in the manufacturing–wholesale–retail chain or sequence. In general, the retailer is involved in the procurement of a larger variety of items than the wholesaler or the manufacturer, depending upon the type of products involved. However, usually the buyer at the retail and the wholesale level is less concerned about the scientific and technical aspects of purchasing.

As we described the purchasing function in the previous chapter, we concentrated more on the role of purchasing in a manufacturing setting in order to illustrate the diverse nature of the positions involved in the procurement of products and services. As someone investigating the opportunities in purchasing, you should also be aware of the many opportunities in the wholesale and retail levels of the distribution process. As we describe the many positions available in purchasing in the following pages, keep in the back of your mind that most of these jobs are found at all levels of commerce, from mining the original raw material to stocking the retailer's shelf.

COMPANY ORGANIZATION

One of the simplest methods of understanding the role of purchasing in today's economy is to analyze its position within a typical company or agency organization chart. Within the past five decades, purchasing has gained its rightful spot as a top-level support department reaching the same status as marketing, sales, engineering, finance, and operations. Today purchasing is a vital part of strategic short- and long-term planning and is a major player in every step of the evolution of those plans from concept to reality.

Currently purchasing is viewed as one of the principal roads to follow to achieve top-management levels of responsibilities. Purchasing has a major advantage in that its role in the company's operations demands interrelating with practically every other department and, consequently, purchasing has a greater understanding of the total scope of company activities.

As the organizational chart below illustrates, the purchasing department, in a typical business, reports directly to top management or the CEO and is involved in every part of the business operations that deals with materials, materials handling, and costs. It is this broad range of involvement that provides purchasing with its high internal and external profile.

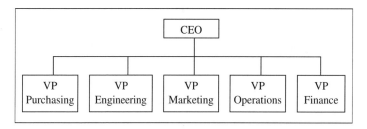

Complex Clerical Positions

Purchasing involves some of the most intricate and complex information handling systems in the entire company, and increasingly, these systems are computer based. Updated data concerning suppliers, sources availability, market conditions, projections, and costs must be available. Paper trails for purchase orders, receiving reports, long-term buying arrangements, invoices, bids, and quotes must be complete and accurate. The bidding or quote process in politically sensitive organizations is extremely complex and visible. In companies using time-delivery systems, the need for accuracy in preparing purchase orders or contracts is critical to the timely delivery of materials or parts. As can be surmised, purchasing administration is detail driven.

These clerical positions, however, provide an excellent opportunity for the beginner to gain an insight into the many facets of purchasing and how these facets relate to other departments. Many of the contacts with finance, production, engineering, accounting, and others involve purchasing administration. In one sense, purchasing is the hub of activity simply because nothing can be accomplished without the proper tools, raw materials, components, merchandise, and services.

The Expediter

A very basic and simple definition of an *expediter* is "one who monitors and controls the flow of materials and services." However, like most simple definitions, this one does not do justice to the importance or the complexity of this function. Once the purchase has been finalized, it is the expediter's job to ensure that the conditions of the commitment or contract are adhered to. Especially for organizations that do not, as a matter of policy, maintain large inventories or raw materials or parts and who depend upon delivery of necessary products or services being made at the proper time and place during the production process, the monitoring and control of materials and services is absolutely critical.

The expediter monitors a purchase from the time it is committed by following up on the purchase orders with the vendor to ensure that everything is on schedule. Sometimes he or she visits the vendor's facilities to monitor its production schedules to ensure timely deliveries. In many companies, the expediter's responsibilities do not end when the product is delivered. The expediter is also responsible for the handling of materials internally from inventory to production or from central receiving to retail. As noted before, the position of expediter is often used as a training ground because the duties offer the opportunity to gain experience in many aspects of materials handling management.

THE BUYER

The term *buyer* encompasses the widest variety of skills, responsibilities, and technical knowledge requirements of any job title in business and industry today. As in many other occupations, the buying or purchasing function is becoming increasingly specialized, and consequently, lateral transfer from one buying specialty to another is not as common as it might have been a decade or two previously. To illustrate the variety and the complexity of the buyer's position, we will look at the buyer's job in three broad categories of organizational activity: wholesale/retail, manufacturing/industrial, and service/governmental.

Wholesale/Retail Buyers

In reality, the retail buyer is at the end of the entire manufacturing, distribution, and merchandising chain. It is the retail buyer who purchases goods from the wholesaler or, occasionally, directly from the manufacturer for resale to the general public. The retail buyer must know potential customers, their likes and dislikes, their spending habits, and their motivation for buying. Equally as important, buyers must be able to identify trends and fads and to project the longevity of the swings of consumer preference. In such industries as clothing, toys, fashion accessories, and cosmetics, misjudgments on the part of both wholesale and retail buyers can be disastrous. The pages of the history of retailing are filled with the stories of those who misread consumer demands.

Retail buyers are market driven. They study market research data constantly to track the direction of consumer demand. They review sales records to identify the winners and the losers, and they are always seeking information about new products.

Both retail and wholesale merchandise buyers must constantly monitor economic conditions, regionally and nationally, to determine potential market strength, since this information will influence the size of an order. Inventory that does not sell is the recurring nightmare of every retail and wholesale buyer. Both types of buyers must thoroughly understand the merchandising system, how merchandise is priced, discounting practices, and shelf life.

Retail buyers are in constant contact with many others involved in retailing. They work with wholesalers to identify potential sources of supply, store executives to iron out delivery and promotional problems, and the advertising department to discuss sales promotions. They deal with salespeople to keep in touch with customer likes and dislikes and, equally important, the hints of developing trends in style or fashion.

Retail and wholesale buyers must be quality conscious, particularly in today's competitive marketplace. In order to buy for both high- and low-end markets, buyers must have a basic technical knowledge of the products to be purchased. They must also be aware of the various government regulations concerning labeling, product safety, prohibited ingredients, and misrepresentation.

The life of a buyer in the retail or wholesale trade is often fast paced. The volume and the variety of products to be purchased require that decisions be made rapidly and sometimes under great pressure. Mistakes in anticipating the whims of the consuming public can be very costly, and consequently, most buyers are very conscious of the risks involved. Generally there is considerable travel involved, as many of the purchase decisions are made at trade events, fashion shows, or product fairs. Buyers often have to visit production facilities to inspect quality control functions and to confirm product specifications. Often at both shows and on-site inspections, quasi-social functions are involved, requiring the buyer to exercise good judgment and resourcefulness in maintaining an objective and professional attitude.

Manufacturing/Industrial Buyer

Within the manufacturing/industrial environment, the buyer is directly involved in the acquisition of a variety of products, raw materials, and services used in the production process. A partial list of purchases may include such items as components, finished parts, chemicals, electrical and electronic parts and equipment, computer hardware and software, metals, plastics, construction equipment and materials, vehicles, and fuels. It is not at all unusual for a buyer in a larger company to specialize in the purchase of one category of items. In the raw material and commodity areas, for example, buyers specialize in grains, cattle, steel stock, and other high-volume products requiring an extensive knowledge of both the items and the markets.

Another area involving a high degree of specialization is the procurement of services such as insurance, maintenance contracts, pest control, or custodial services. Usually the buyer must have not only an extensive knowledge of the service but also must be familiar with basic contract law.

Generally it is the buyer who is in close contact with engineering and operations in order to develop specifications, supply requirements, delivery schedules, and quality levels. Again, a knowledge of the technical aspects of the product or service is extremely important because the buyer must translate information about the required product into descriptions and processes clearly understood by potential suppliers. Since in many cases buying products by some type of brand name is not desirable or even possible, the written specification of the required product becomes the only basis of common understanding between the buyer and the supplier.

The buyer, in cooperation with engineering and operations, is also responsible for establishing quality standards and criteria. Often, when buying component parts or basic items such as wire or metal stock, the specifications will state the materials and the processes that must be used by the supplier to ensure that quality standards are met. The buyer is also often responsible for developing quality inspection systems at the receiving point. It is not unusual for quality inspections to take place at the supplier's facilities before the purchased items are delivered to the user.

A common misconception about a buyer's job portrays an image of a person who does nothing all day but interview salespeople. Actually, most buyers actively pursue their sources of supply. They discover new sources through trade shows, industry meetings with others in the same business, association meetings, or by reviewing product listings. Personal interviews are an essential part of the buying process, so buyers generally have excellent listening skills. They know the right questions to ask and become proficient in the interpretation of body language. Buyers obviously must be good negotiators because, throughout the buyer–supplier relationship, some aspect of the transaction such as offer, counteroffer, compromise, acceptance, or denial is being discussed.

The buyer's job is not over once the order is placed. Vendor performance in terms of quality, quantity, and delivery must continuously be evaluated and compared. In those companies with low or even without inventory systems, vendor reliability is critical to the production process. A vendor's lack of performance can shut down a production line.

Most buyers protect their positions by maintaining alternate sources of supply for every item required. Often they split orders or alternate suppliers to ensure that they do not have all their eggs in one basket. Vendors go out of business, have fires or natural disasters, strikes, or many other types of mishaps that prevent them from meeting delivery schedules, and buyers must be prepared for every type of emergency. Although there is a trend in many companies to reduce the number of suppliers, buyers must be certain that their primary vendor poses little or no risk to the production process.

Buyers must have the ability to read the markets. The future availability of products and commodities will have an obvious impact on a company's short- and long-term planning. In today's economy, forecasting the market and the supply has international implications. Companies are increasingly becoming partially or totally dependent upon foreign markets for raw material and component parts, particularly in the electronics and appliance fields. Consequently, some buyers are expected to travel abroad frequently.

A continuous interface with the sales department is important, particularly in those industries involved in customized products or component parts manufacturing. Often the customers require that component parts be manufactured according to their specifications, which will in turn dictate a specific material or process.

Perhaps the most important requirement for a successful buyer is a standard of ethics that is beyond question. Obviously he or she is in a position to commit enormous sums of money, and some suppliers offer tempting inducements to swing the odds of getting the order in their favor. Buyers develop reputations very rapidly simply because salespeople talk, and the buyer that earns a reputation for being objective, fair, and knowledgeable has the opportunity to develop long-term business relationships with reputable suppliers. Suppliers will negotiate more fairly if they are assured they will not have to pay hidden inducement costs.

Although no one will deny that product knowledge is essential to the success of a buyer, a recent survey of purchasing executives revealed that the ability to develop long-term interpersonal relationships was among the top prerequisites for attaining success in the purchasing field.

Service/Government Buyers

The key factor in the field of service and government buying is the source of the money used for purchases. In most cases, the source of the funds will be either from the taxpayer, membership dues, or charitable donations. In all cases, the source is public and highly visible, a fact that demands that purchasing systems also be public and visible. Particularly in government purchasing, since the sellers are also taxpayers, the buyers are under a unique pressure to ensure that the system is fair and allows all qualified sellers to compete. Because of the extreme sensitivity to public scrutiny and criticism, most government buying systems are based on a highly structured formal quote or bid procedure.

The formal bid system is essentially defensive in nature—defensive in the sense that it is perceived to be completely fair and open by all of those interested in selling products to a government entity and by taxpayers assuming a watchdog status. The high visibility requires the government buyer to emphasize two important aspects of the buying process: the product or service specification and the ability of the bidder or seller to perform. While a nongovernment buyer is often free to use his or her judgment and experience as to the qualifications of a potential vendor, the government buyer must base his or her decisions on predetermined and publicized standards or criteria.

Specifications are extremely important in service and government buying. Often the buyer is required to accept the lowest bid, and, therefore, many of the intangibles that can influence a decision in the private sector cannot be considered by the government buyer unless it is stated as a bidding requirement.

The bidding documents, consequently, are usually much more detailed in terms of both the product or service and the minimum qualifications of the bidder. Often the opening of the bids are public affairs during which most of the bidders are present and the award of the contract is publicly announced.

Because of the highly sensitive nature of service and government purchasing, documentation of every step of the buying process is essential. In most cases, this documentation is a matter of public record and, therefore, is accessible to anyone interested in the process.

Government agencies may also impose formal bidding requirements upon their contractors. This, in turn, imposes a responsibility upon the private sector buyer to follow government procedures.

Government buying requires a sense of integrity and fairness equal to, if not exceeding, other buying classifications, principally because of the possibility of extreme political pressure. Although most systems are designed to insulate the buyer from these pressures, the buyer still must be sensitive to their existence.

THE PURCHASE ANALYST

The position of *purchase analyst* is primarily a research function requiring a thorough knowledge of both products and the markets. By analyzing various types of statistical data, the purchase analyst determines the feasibility of purchasing certain types of products, establishes an acceptable pricing structure, and projects pricing trends. This position is usually found in larger organizations, and the data generated by the analyst are used in strategic planning and the actual purchasing process.

Both short-term and long-term strategic planning requires extensive information about potential markets, availability of raw materials and components, production cost analysis, market segmentation, and pricing trend projections. The purchase analyst maintains a continuous relationship with suppliers and the markets in general to develop a scenario of current and projected conditions affecting the company's position. The position is data driven but also requires considerable independent judgment in the analysis of the data.

The purchase analyst is also one of the primary sources of cost and pricing data for the buyers during their negotiations with potential suppliers. The purchase analyst position often requires considerable interaction with all segments of the market in order to obtain the broad range of necessary information.

THE PROCUREMENT ENGINEER

The procurement engineer is found primarily in the manufacturing portion of business activities. The position requires the ability to analyze technical data as they relate to the development of both preliminary and final specifications. Often this person is involved with engineering personnel in the development of performance criteria and standards. He or she may inspect suppliers' facilities to determine their capabilities to produce products according to specifications and may also be involved in collecting data on short- and long-term materials availability.

The procurement engineer is also a troubleshooter, in that he or she participates in the resolution of problems that involve the suppliers, buyers, inspectors, and production personnel. These problems often arise when existing contracts must be modified because of unforeseen circumstances and consequently involve all levels of the materials handling and production process.

The scope of the duties of a procurement engineer usually go beyond the buying process, in that he or she may be involved in many aspects of plant operations. Examples of such involvement may be the standardization of parts or equipment, product or process rework, materials salvage, and the use of equipment used in plant operations.

Obviously, the position requires someone with a technical background. However, the person occupying the position must have a thorough knowledge of purchasing techniques and the ability to interrelate with all levels of both the company and the suppliers. In order to arrive at workable solutions, the procurement engineer, in his or her troubleshooting function, must have a complete understanding of the acquisition and the production processes.

THE PURCHASING MANAGER

The term *manager* covers a multitude of duties and responsibilities in the purchasing field. Because purchasing is an active function within almost every type of a business or organization, for profit or nonprofit, there is always someone who must oversee and manage that function. How the management is structured depends on a variety of factors: the size of the company, the product or service involved, centralized or decentralized system, continuous standardized or custom production, the amount of subcontracting involved, the variety and number of components or raw materials required. These factors dictate the number of levels of managers and the nature of their responsibilities. In a complex aircraft manufacturing company producing a variety of aircraft for both military and civilian markets, there may be a multitiered management structure consisting of section, group, and project managers along with specialty administrators who manage support activities such as major subcontracting or traffic. In smaller and less complex companies or organizations, the purchasing manager may do some of the buying in addition to supervising assistant buyers and clerical personnel. In retailing, managers are often identified with product classifications. A large department store chain, for example, may have managers for housewares, clothing, cosmetics, perfumes, and sporting goods. Again, these managers may purchase some of the products while also supervising other buyers and clerical personnel.

The broad responsibilities of purchasing managers are quite similar despite the variety of size and complexity. The purchasing manager must operate the department in conformance with general operating policy established by top management. He or she is responsible for meeting deadlines, scheduling and assigning work, supervising staff, and establishing training and development programs for employees. Often each level or classification of managers is given dollar limits as to size of purchases or contracts that they can approve. For example, section managers may approve up to five million dollars, group managers up to fifteen million dollars, and so on. Managers may also be identified by a project; that is, they may be responsible for all purchasing activities for only one item that is produced by the company. After setting up the procedures necessary for procurement for that product, the manager may then be assigned to a new project.

The multitiered management structure is important to the goal-oriented individual because the various levels represent the promotional or advancement track. Each level is the testing and training ground for the next, and since most organizations prefer to promote from within in the purchasing field, an individual may easily set goals in terms of both levels and times. The project manager may also make advancement goals since promotions are often based on the size of the project. For example, a project manager may graduate from a five-million-dollar project to a twenty-five-million-dollar project, and salary is usually adjusted accordingly.

Purchasing managers may report to one of several positions within the company or organization. In larger companies, purchasing managers may report to the director or vice-president of purchasing or materials management. In smaller companies, they may report directly to the CEO or president, the general manager, director of operations, or the manufacturing or plant manager.

In educational institutions and health-care facilities, the purchasing manager is most often a position within the business office or administration. Unlike the industrial or manufacturing fields, it is not unusual to find purchasing managers reporting to the chief fiscal officer of the institution. Seldom will you find institutional purchasing managers arranged in multitiered structures. They are more often classified according to product or service categories, such as food service, maintenance, medical supplies, furniture, books.

Regardless of the field—manufacturing, institutional, or retailing—purchasing managers usually serve on a variety of committees. Most are involved in one or more of the following: production, budget, capital spending, human resources, safety, planning, policy, standardization. At this level, practically all committees are internal or staff committees usually reporting to the chief executive officer or to the president.

THE HEAD OF PURCHASING

The top-ranked purchasing position is usually given the title of vice-president of purchasing, director of purchasing or procurement, or director of materials management. As head of the purchasing function, he or she is an important part of the management and executive team taking part in almost all aspects of corporate or organizational strategic planning as well as the direction of day-to-day operations. The position involves direct participation in the development and the implementation of operating policies, usually through membership on both board of director and staff committees. As either advisors or members of board of director committees (committees reporting directly to the chairperson of the board), the head of the purchasing function has a direct input into long-term strategic planning.

In educational and health-care institutions, where the administrative and academic or medical activities are apt to be separated more than in the industrial or manufacturing fields, the head of the purchasing function usually reports to the chief administrator or president or to the vice president or director of administration. In this field, purchasing is considered to be a support service, and those working in purchasing are less apt to be involved with long-term strategic planning, except when such planning involves substantial expansion of facilities or major changes in the use of the existing physical plant. As the primary source of purchasing policy, the purchasing director must be ultrasensitive to the public relations aspects of procurement, particularly if the institution is partially or completely supported by taxpayers.

In the field of wholesaling and retailing, the purchasing function is an essential part of the company's purpose and activities. In a business activity that consists almost entirely of buying and selling, half of the emphasis must be on buying and the other half must be on sales and marketing, making the purchasing or buying function part of practically every dollar earned by the company. Unlike the manufacturing plant, whose income is derived from a product, or the institution whose income is derived from a service, the retailer and the wholesaler must obtain their profits from the difference between the purchase price and the selling price. Therefore, corporate planning and policy revolve around these two functions.

The retail and wholesale buying function is directly driven by market projections, resulting in an extremely close working relationship with sales and marketing.

A VARIETY OF OPPORTUNITIES

There are few, if any, business or organizational activities that do not involve purchasing of some type of product or service. As you can see from the preceding pages, the terms *buying, purchasing,* and *procuring* involve an incredible variety of applications, each requiring different experience, knowledge, and personality types. The potential for a satisfying career in purchasing is enormous, especially considering the choices that are available. The following chapters are designed to help you make the right choice for yourself within the field of purchasing.

CHAPTER 3

OPPORTUNITIES IN PURCHASING

As someone who is in the process of investigating various possible career directions, you probably fall into one of the following two categories:

1. The career beginner: The career beginner is someone in college trying to decide on a major, someone who has just graduated and is trying to decide where to apply and in which field, or someone who has been out of high school for some time and has made the decision to find a position that has an on-the-job training potential and a chance for advancement.

2. The career changer: The career changer is a person who has been out of college for several years and is headed in a career direction that is not suited to him or her anymore. This person may be in a job in which he or she has reached a plateau or a dead end. Sometimes the career changer has decided to return to school to finish or supplement his or her education to prepare to enter another career field. The career changer may also be a person who has been out of the job market for an extended period of time and has job skills that are now obsolete.

Whatever your situation, you must first determine what you want your new career direction to do for you. Ultimately, you must also decide what you can do for the potential employer; however, job satisfaction is a two-way street. The employer gains when you meet its needs, and you gain when the employer meets your needs, and seldom does an employer/employee relationship work when mutual needs are not met.

You will have a far greater chance of finding a career that is suitable and productive for both you and your employer if you understand yourself and your needs before you begin the search. The purpose of this chapter is to describe the opportunities and the conditions found in the purchasing field; however, it is up to you to determine whether purchasing is the field for you. For example, your answers to the following questions will help you make that determination as you continue through this chapter and the remainder of the book.

- Are you most comfortable working with other team members or working alone?
- Can you function well if you are under pressure in a fast-paced environment?
- Can you adhere to quality standards and not cut corners? Are you comfortable following guidelines?
- Do you enjoy solving problems, or are you more comfortable following a set routine?
- Can you learn new and complex material rapidly? Do you like being involved with new concepts?
- Are you imaginative?
- Do you have a well-developed sense of humor?
- Are you self-reliant and even tempered? Can you tolerate stress?
- Are you committed to following through on every job?
- Can you work effectively within an organizational structure?
- Can you work with detail and yet understand theory and concepts?
- Do you need the challenge of important and meaningful work?

In addition to psychological needs, which can vary widely between individuals, there are some needs or desires that are common to most. For example, most people want a job that is interesting. Most want good pay and benefits, pleasant working conditions, and the opportunity for advancement. Those of you who have had some experience in the workforce also want supportive management and an opportunity to provide ideas and input. Many want to work at a job that is meaningful and produces tangible results. All of these job factors are important when making a career choice.

As we investigate purchasing as a potential career path, we will first look at some of the more obvious characteristics, such as compensation levels, benefits, and working conditions. Keep in mind, however, that this career field is multifaceted and that many of the job factors will depend upon the size and location of the organization, the type of activity (manufacturing, service, or wholesale/retail), the level of technology, and the economic environment.

COMPENSATION

The term *compensation* for the purposes of this discussion is limited to salary and bonuses and does not include the value of some of the perks that may be offered. In general, the salaries in purchasing are in line with other positions at comparable levels in an organizational structure and, like these other positions, there can be a wide range depending on the industry and the location. There is also a gender gap, especially at the senior management level, but this gap is gradually narrowing.

United States

Generally, male and female graduates with a bachelor's degree can expect a salary in the mid-twenties, but as a person advances and gains more experience, the range of salaries begins to widen. Those looking at purchasing as a long-term career will be interested in some of the results of the latest annual salary survey conducted by *Purchasing Magazine.* The survey is categorized by factors that most often impact basic salary levels.

INDUSTRY GROUP

The highest paying industry is the stone, glass, and clay group with an annual average salary of $64,000. Some other industry examples are:

Chemicals	$61,800
Energy	55,100
Public utilities	54,300
Wholesale	49,500
Misc. manufacturing	45,900
Financial services	44,000

EXPERIENCE

As in most professions, experience in purchasing leads to increased compensation. The purchasing executive does not, however, begin to earn more than the average salary until after the tenth year of experience. The average salaries based on experience are:

3 years or less	$40,500
4–6 years	43,000
7–10 years	46,100
11–15 years	52,400
Over 15 years	59,300

EDUCATION

The results of the *Purchasing Magazine* survey leave little doubt about the value of education in determining salary levels. College graduates hold the highest ranking positions, have the greatest responsibilities, work for the largest companies, and earn the highest compensation. The average salaries based on education are:

No degree	$41,800
BS (liberal arts)	49,400
BS (business)	51,500
BS (technical)	57,400
MBA	68,100
Other graduate	53,700

JOB TITLE

It is important to note that job titles for the same responsibilities will differ from one company to another. Based on the job titles reported by the participating companies, the average salaries are:

Buyer	$35,000
Senior buyer	46,200
Purchasing agent	41,200
Purchasing manager	55,400
Materials manager	55,300
Materials director	85,100
Purchasing director	75,800
VP, purchasing	105,000

The salary ranges for the various titles is quite wide. For example, among those participating in the survey the highest salary for

a purchasing agent was $108,000; for a materials manager—
$148,000; for a purchasing manager—$213,000; for a purchasing
director—$200,000; and for a VP, purchasing—$310,000.

There has been a decided trend in recent years in all executive
ranks to use a bonus as a significant part of total compensation,
and the purchasing executive is no exception. Forty-four percent of
all those participating in the survey received bonuses as part of
their compensation, although the size of the bonus varied considerably. Senior executives received bonuses that represented a larger
portion of their total compensation. The average bonus for purchasing vice presidents (VPs) was 23 percent of base salary, while
those buyers who received bonuses averaged just 8 percent of base.

Professional purchasing officers may be certified as Certified
Purchasing Managers by the National Purchasing Managers Association, and these certifications do have a positive effect upon salary levels. For example, professionals with certification earned an
average of $60,300, while those without certification averaged
$48,000.

Canada

Salary ranges also vary in Canada according to location and
type of industry, although the widest difference is between the private and the governmental/institutional sectors. The public sector
organizations are adversely impacted by significantly reduced
funding, and consequently, salary increases have flattened.

The highest average salaries are found in the provinces of British
Columbia and Alberta ($52,000 plus), while the lowest are found in
Quebec ($51,700) and the Atlantic ($44,300) areas. The type of
organization is also important, as can be seen by the following:

Institutions	$45,200
Trade	47,200

Government	47,600
Manufacturing	50,900
Services	52,300
Natural resources	57,400

As in the United States, the amount of education affects average salary levels in Canada. However, the Canadian study, unlike the U.S. report, does not separate university graduates and post graduates. The average salaries according to educational levels in Canada are:

High School	$47,500
Trade/Technical	56,400
Some post secondary	49,000
Community college graduate	49,100
University graduate	53,600

Canada uses the same basic job titles as the United States but job descriptions may differ from one organization to another for the same job title. Average salaries (and bonuses) per job title are:

Title	Average Salary	Bonus percent
VP/Director, purchasing	$71,300	12.0%
Materials manager	57,400	6.0%
Purchasing manager	56,100	8.5%
Purchasing agent	44,600	4.7%
Senior buyer	46,800	5.0%
Other buyer	41,700	4.3%

(Canadian salary information is based on the *1996 Annual Purchasing Profile,* a joint project of *Modern Purchasing Magazine* and The Purchasing Management Association of Canada.)

Canada also has certification programs available sponsored by the Purchasing Management Association of Canada. Their certification, Certified Professional Purchaser/Approvisionneur Professionel Agree (CPP/a.p.a.), has a significant impact upon earning levels. Those with the CPP/a.p.a. earn 26 percent more than those who do not have the certification.

WORKING CONDITIONS

Since purchasing is a critical function in every type of business or government activity, working conditions in terms of working environment, activity, and variety are usually excellent. There is ample opportunity to travel and considerable interaction with coworkers and suppliers at all levels. Because of the nature of the job, there is also considerable independence of action—supervision tends to be general rather than close.

Since new products and services are being developed constantly, and methods of doing business are continuously changing, most companies offer many opportunities for education and self-improvement through seminars, training classes, and other educational programs. Most organizations maintain easy access to professional associations like the National Association of Purchasing Management and their state affiliates. These associations sponsor numerous conferences and seminars at local, state, and national levels and act as conduits for information of concern to the purchasing professional.

JOB STABILITY

Purchasing positions tend to be very stable, much more so than positions in sales or manufacturing. Again, because of the nature of the work, purchasing is more insulated against the ups and downs of business activity because the numbers may change but the products and services still must be procured.

Job stability is also enhanced because of the complexity of the job. A purchasing manager or a buyer has developed a knowledge of the market and the potential suppliers that is not easily replaced. The fact that most higher levels of positions in purchasing are filled by promotions from within also contributes to general job stability. Again, the exposure to all levels of management and functions of the organization make the purchasing official an indispensable part of the team.

ADVANCEMENT

Organizations tend to promote from within the purchasing field. However, because of their knowledge of internal operations of the organization as a whole, purchasing officials are often promoted to other high-level positions on the top management team. In fact, many people enter purchasing as a means to advance into general management.

Larger organizations have numerous advancement opportunities within the ranks of middle management. Purchasing managers advance from section managers to group or project managers and then go on to divisional responsibilities.

PROFILES OF PURCHASING PROFESSIONALS

Recently, the Center for Advanced Purchasing Studies published a report that included much information about the background of the chief purchasing officials (CPOs) who participated in their survey. This information is very valuable to those wishing to make a career in purchasing because it gives a clear picture of the education and experience necessary to reach the top of this career field. The study included both U.S. and Canadian companies.

Although the question of how much education is necessary for a career in purchasing is still controversial, there is a definite trend towards firms requiring a bachelor's degree. The survey among CPOs indicated that 56 percent of those based in the United States had bachelor's degrees and, in Canada, 58 percent had bachelor's degrees. Forty percent of U.S.-based CPOs had graduate degrees, compared to 19 percent in Canada. Overall, 58 percent majored in business and 19 percent majored in engineering. The most common graduate degree was an MBA, although there were quite a few with a master's in Economics or Engineering.

A quick look at the occupational background of the CPO participants indicated that most had been in purchasing for some time, but a significant number had entered the field from other functions such as operations/manufacturing, engineering, marketing, and finance. It is necessary to bear in mind that an academic concentration in purchasing has only been available in colleges for a little over a decade, so most of the current group of CPOs gained their knowledge through experience.

Purchasing professionals also spend considerable time serving on standing and ad-hoc committees such as production, human resources, management, finance, and operations. Again, serving on such a broad range of committees provides the purchasing professional with an overview of organizational policy and procedures.

Ninety percent of purchasing professionals travel as part of their job. They average ten trips per year, although some may travel in excess of 100,000 miles per year. Reasons for the travel include investigating supply facilities, negotiating with suppliers, and attending trade shows.

Eighty-seven percent indicated that, if given the chance to start over, they would again choose purchasing as a career. The level of satisfaction is very high, much higher than most other career fields. Consequently, we must assume that a purchasing career meets a high percentage of the needs and expectations of those involved.

PREPARING FOR A CAREER IN PURCHASING

Consider first that practically every organization in both the private and public sectors requires the purchase of some type of product or service. Consider second the vast array of products and services involved, and you will understand why there is not a standard educational and work experience background that is judged to be the best for the purchasing field. Each position demands a different background and knowledge although certain personality characteristics are considered essential for most purchasing positions.

Personality Characteristics

The National Association of Purchasing Managers (NAPM) lists the following characteristics as being most desirable for potential purchasing professionals:

- integrity
- dependability
- industriousness
- cooperative nature
- tact
- an ability to learn
- an ability to work on details
- mechanical aptitude
- good interpersonal relationship and communication skills

- an inquiring mind
- a sense of value
- high ethical standards.

To that list could be added:

- sense of humor
- the ability to tolerate stress
- the ability to make comparative judgments
- the ability to think, write, and speak intelligently and logically

There are some psychological and personality traits that seem to be consistently valuable, regardless of the type of purchasing classification. For example, most purchasing positions require much interaction with other departments and suppliers. Consequently, the persons in those positions must be group motivated—they must receive satisfaction and incentive by working closely with others. They must be supportive and socially self-confident, completely comfortable in their role as a team player.

Since much of their time is involved in the role of negotiator, they must be assertive without being overbearing, they must be emotionally stable, and they must not let their ego get in the way of their common sense. Also, they must be able to cope with situational pressures.

Some of the time they will be working alone, during buying trips, facility and process inspections, and conferences. They must be self-motivated, disciplined, and organized.

Much of their work involves problem solving. Consequently, they must think in abstract, conceptual terms; have excellent analytical skills; and be able to communicate ideas or points of view verbally and in writing.

Normal career progression involves management responsibilities at some point. Therefore, the purchasing professional must be even tempered and consistent in mood. He or she must also have excellent management skills.

Since the purchasing professional often has access to sensitive information concerning company operations, he or she must have a strong sense of loyalty and corporate ethics.

Purchasing professionals control large sums of money. Often this control places them in a position of being offered inducements for preferential treatment. They must have impeccable standards of ethical conduct and be fair and honest with a strong sense of integrity.

In summation, the purchasing professional is someone occupying a position of trust, a position critical to the success of a company or organization. The demands of the professional are many and require someone emotionally stable. Those considering purchasing as a career must be prepared to make a commitment to the high ethical standards of the profession.

Recommended Educational Background

There is a definite trend toward the requirement of a bachelor's degree for beginning positions in purchasing. The emergence of majors in purchasing or materials management at several prominent colleges and universities reinforces the trend. However, no one type of educational background is appropriate for all purchasing positions, and the lack of a bachelor's degree does not mean that the doors are closed to those who have significant related work experience.

An educational background in purchasing provides broad theoretical knowledge of the field and how it relates to business or organizational activities. Further knowledge of the product or services is a matter of training or work experience in most cases.

For those entering college or in the process of selecting their majors, the National Association of Purchasing Managers offers the following suggestions.

The ideal college curriculum consists of a concentration in business administration with a major in purchasing or materials management. Realizing, however, that many colleges do not offer such majors, the NAPM suggests the following courses:

- Basic Economics
- Principles of Accounting
- Business Communications
- Commercial Law
- Statistics and Quantitative Methods
- Computer Applications in Business
- Business Organization and Management
- Managerial Finance
- Fundamentals of Marketing
- Marketing Research
- Production Planning and Control
- Cost Accounting

The NAPM also suggests the following specific courses, if they are available:

- Principles of Purchasing
- Negotiation and Cost Analysis
- Contract Administration
- Purchasing Research
- Purchasing and Materials Management Strategy
- Government Purchasing
- Materials Management
- Traffic Management

It is also strongly suggested that a person take courses in his or her areas of strongest interest. Those wishing to become involved with purchasing in manufacturing may want to take some engineering courses while others who are interested in the retail area may take courses in foods, textiles, or merchandising.

Again, one of the principal requirements for a purchasing professional is a thorough knowledge of the products or services that he or she is concerned with. Almost without exception, purchasers gain this knowledge through a variety of ways after they have received their formal education. In a larger company or organization, they may be assigned to a formal training program in which they will be systematically transferred from one department to another as they gain experience in many of the functions performed by the purchasing department. Other companies use the on-the-job training method, in which new employees observe buyers at work or assist them under close supervision.

There are some positions in purchasing or buying in which adequate knowledge of the product can be gained only through extensive experience. A cattle buyer is a good example of a person whose knowledge cannot be gained through formal education or rigid training programs. Only years of experience in the field can provide the ability to make sound judgments as to the comparative value of cattle.

Another valuable source of training and continuing education is the trade associations. The National Association of Purchasing Management, for example, offers conferences, seminars, and workshops continuously and also offers a professional certification program by which one can earn the designation of certified purchasing manager. Practically every product line, from electronics to fancy foods,is represented by a trade association, and most hold national and regional trade shows where hundreds of suppliers exhibit their products. These trade shows provide the buyers with the opportunity to see many competitive products at one time with a minimum of travel. Individual industries, such as home builders, are also represented by trade associations. They also hold national and regional conventions and trade shows and invite suppliers of products relating to their industry to exhibit. Again, buyers have an opportunity to view hundreds or even thousands of products and services under the same roof.

It is not unusual for people interested in purchasing in certain fields, such as wholesaling or retailing, to intentionally enter the industry as a member of a department other than purchasing. A potential fashion buyer, for example, may want to gain experience in textiles, clothing design, and merchandising before applying for a position as a buyer. This method of entering the purchasing field is designed to enhance the buyer's knowledge of the products and, equally as important, the market.

From one point of view, the purchasing field offers something for everyone. The products and services are so diverse, the working conditions so varied, and the knowledge and expertise required covers such a broad range, that whether you are interested in chemicals or corn, some aspect of purchasing should appeal to you.

CHAPTER 4

THE PURCHASING PROFESSION IN THE TWENTY-FIRST CENTURY

As noted before, the purchasing profession, like most other business-oriented professions, is in the midst of significant change. Its role in the management hierarchy is expanding and taking on new dimensions that, in turn, will impact the skills and training necessary for purchasing professions to function in the future. These anticipated changes will present a challenge to both industry and educational institutions to provide on-the-job training and formal education resources in order to meet new skill and technical requirements.

There have been several surveys involving current purchasing managers and executive officers that attempt to identify trends in business that will affect purchasing during the next decade. According to these surveys, the following areas will be most susceptable to change.

COMPUTERIZATION

Computer literacy will be absolutely necessary in most aspects of purchasing. A study by James Carbone for *Purchasing Magazine* showed that already over half of the buyers surveyed have access to the Internet and the World Wide Web (WWW), and about 80 percent use it frequently in their jobs. Some buyers use the Internet as a research tool accessing supplier catalogs on the Web to locate products and components. Others use it to automate the purchasing process, from sending out requests for quotations to placing purchase orders and tracking orders. E-mail is another area that has seen considerable growth in both the United States and Canada.

PURCHASING STRATEGIES

Studies in the United States and Canada have shown that 80 percent of a buyer's or purchaser's time is spent on 20 percent of the dollars expended. Obviously this statistic has caused considerable concern, and many companies are reengineering their purchasing functions to streamline the process and make them more strategically directed.

One of the strategies is to decentralize the purchasing process in order to allow the using department to make small dollar purchases directly from approved vendors. The vehicles to control and account for these departmental expenditures are corporate purchase cards or general credit cards usually limited to $1,000.00. Like the consumer credit cards, the user or company receives a detailed monthly statement, thus freeing the purchasing department to spend more time on negotiating for big ticket items.

OUTSOURCING

Many companies are turning the management of certain products and services over to qualified suppliers. This process usually results in more longer-term contracts and fewer suppliers, as well as less involvement by buyers or purchasers. This type of business arrangement means a greater emphasis on negotiation and contract administration.

THIRD-PARTY LOGISTICS

As companies continue to downsize to core activities, purchasers are becoming more involved in the contracting out of transportation, distribution, and warehousing functions to third parties. Again, this trend emphasizes negotiating prowess on the part of the purchasing department and actually involves them in functions formerly managed by other departments.

CENTRALIZATION
VERSUS DECENTRALIZATION

As the trend toward corporate mergers and acquisitions continues, the purchasing functions are changing to adapt to larger organizations operating in widespread locations. In some cases purchasing can be accomplished in one centralized location, usually at corporate level, but in many instances, the concentration of purchasing becomes too cumbersome and inefficient. Most large conglomerates are fragmented with operating locations throughout the United States and Canada and even the world. Often these locations are separated into regions that contain any number of individual operations.

Many of these multiunit and multilayered companies are separating the purchasing function according to product and service. Those products unique to one or a few localized operations are purchased locally by staff based at the operating unit, while items and services common to most operations within a region or the company are purchased at the regional or corporate level. High dollar and capital expense items are usually purchased at a centralized corporate level.

This separation or layering of purchasing functions creates numerous middle- and upper-management career opportunities, and oddly, the regional positions often pay better than the corporate level, with positions at the unit level coming in a distant third.

Two recent studies have been completed that outline the directions the purchasing functions will be following over the next decade. The first, *Purchasing Education and Training,* by Michael G. Kolchin, DBA, CPM, and Larry Giunipero, Ph.D., CPM, for the Center for Advanced Purchasing Studies, concentrates on the training and resources that must be provided to prepare purchasers for the future. According to the study, the ten most important subjects to be provided are as follows:

- Total cost analysis
- Negotiation strategies and techniques
- Supplier partnership management
- Ethical conduct
- Supplier evaluation
- Quality techniques
- Purchasing strategy and planning
- Price/cost analysis
- Electronic data interchange
- Interpersonal communication

The second study was conducted by Harold E. Fearon, Ph.D., CPM, Director of the Center for Advanced Purchasing Studies, and Michiel R. Leenders, DBA, FPMAC, Purchasing Management Association of Canada. The study was titled, *Purchasing Organizational Roles and Responsibilities.* Their study highlighted the increasing use of cross-functional teams that involve not only other departments within the organization but also customers and suppliers. This trend confirms the opinions of many others that purchasing will depend upon even more skills in negotiating, team building and understanding company goals. A diverse background of education and experience will be required as the need to work closely with other departments increases.

CHAPTER 5

PROFILES OF SUCCESSFUL PURCHASING EXECUTIVES

According to the National Association of Purchasing Management, there are approximately 550,000 people in the field of purchasing today in the United States. Consider, however, that every product, every part of every product, and every service is bought and sold from one to four times before it is actually used, and you might think that those figures are understated. It is, however, easy to understand why the field of purchasing is evolving into a highly specialized occupational area, particularly in the United States. Simply stated, society is driven by competition, and everyone wants a piece of the pie. Consequently, every time you want a product or a service, you have a choice, a complete range of quality and price. The art of purchasing is choosing the right quality and price to fit your needs. This is oversimplification, but consider buyers in a country whose manufacturing and importing is controlled by the government. Their jobs are simple because there is little or no choice. They are order placers, not buyers. Therefore, it is correct to assume that the more choices there are, the more professional and sophisticated the buyers must be.

The next question must be how does the professional and sophisticated buyer select one product or service among the many that are offered? It is at this point that the difference in purchasing or buying methods becomes apparent. Each industry has its own methods and style. One industry may emphasize product knowledge, and another may utilize engineering departments or technical committees. Government agencies stress purchasing procedures. Each industry has its own internal goals, and its purchasing methods must be designed to meet those goals.

In this and the following chapters, we will discuss the peculiar requirements of a variety of industry classifications and how each demands distinct educational and experience backgrounds and, in many cases, different personality types. You will find that there are fundamental reasons why each classification employs its own purchasing system and why purchasers in different industries often have unique relationships with management and other departments. Pay particular attention to the personality requirements of each industry, because the more compatible you are, the better your chances are for success.

There is probably no better way to illustrate the diverse nature of the purchasing career field than to actually describe how some purchasing professionals entered the field and how they progressed during their career. Because of the rapid evolution of the purchasing function, few of those profiled on the following pages actually entered the workforce intending to make purchasing a lifelong career. Typically, most started in entry-level positions in a variety of industries—some out of college, others out of high school or trade schools. Many with high school diplomas or less than four years of college went back to school while working to obtain more general knowledge in business; however, few actually enrolled in courses relating to purchasing, simply because these types of courses were not generally available.

Since the purchasing field has been and still is growing rapidly, the demand for skilled purchasing personnel has exceeded the supply, thus creating ample opportunity for advancement. You will notice that some of the profiles reflect how continuous growth has affected the rate of promotions and how the purchasing professionals have been able to grow with their companies.

PURCHASING AGENT
FOR A MAJOR HOTEL CHAIN

Christopher Daniels is an excellent example of a purchasing professional who learned the tools of his trade by working his way up from an entry-level position in the hospitality industry. Originally hired as a houseman, within a relatively short time he asked to be transferred into the purchasing department as an assistant purchasing agent. The request was granted, and he began on-the-job training in the buying of cleaning and office supplies. He then became involved with the food and beverage purchasing. After several years as an assistant, he then accepted a position with another major chain as an executive steward, working closely with the dining and banquet departments. It was a high-volume operation, and he soon accumulated a working knowledge of food and beverage production and service. When the position of purchasing agent for the same hotel became available, he was given the job.

As in most hotel chains, the purchasing of the furnishings and major equipment is the function of the design and engineering departments at the corporate level. Consequently, Daniels's primary buying responsibilities involve the food and beverage service, housekeeping, and office operations. Although the basic purchasing policies are also developed at the corporate level, the very nature of the products purchased at the hotel level requires developing procedures that will meet the needs of each individual hotel.

From Daniels's viewpoint, the feedback from the people who use the products he buys is very important. Although he is very knowledgeable about materials, concentrations, and the physical or chemical composition of the products, the users must also be able to understand the proper application of the product. Because most supply items are manufactured and, therefore, are reasonably consistent in quality, only a reasonable amount of product knowledge and evaluation is necessary. The purchasing of food products, however, requires extensive product knowledge and a complete understanding of market forces. Market conditions and availability of products can change overnight, forcing changes in menus or the substitution of one product for another.

Food products also require continuous receiving inspections and vendor evaluations to ensure that they meet quality specifications. Daniels is very aware of the fact that poor quality can dramatically increase food costs and customer complaints.

Although most of the knowledge required in his job can only be gained through experience, Daniels now feels that it is time to go back to school to gain more knowledge in management and supervision. When asked to identify the most important skill needed in hotel purchasing, Daniels quickly replied, "The ability to communicate under all types of circumstances and still remain even tempered and outgoing. I spend most of my working day dealing with various departments of the hotel, the guests, and, of course, the vendors. Although I must maintain good working relationships, I must also discipline myself to be very conscious of time."

PURCHASING UNIT SUPERVISOR IN BANKING

The purchasing department of this major banking chain is headed by the manager of purchasing, a position generally considered to be at the vice-president level. Reporting to him are three unit supervisors specializing in the following areas: office furniture, office products, and warehousing/distribution. These three positions buy, warehouse, and distribute products for over six hundred branch banks and two corporate headquarters. Mark Held is the purchasing unit supervisor in charge of purchasing office products of seven to eight thousand different types. His total purchase volume adds up to seven to ten million dollars annually.

Held currently has an associate's degree and is working toward his bachelor's. Like many purchasing officials, his first full-time job was related to the purchasing field but did not actually involve buying. As an inventory control clerk in a wood products factory, his primary responsibility involved control of the raw lumber stock. He then went into retail management but returned to the purchasing field when he became a private label buyer. His next position was as a systems buyer, purchasing point-of-sale equipment for use in retailing. This job gave him the opportunity to become thoroughly familiar with computer systems and supplies, a knowledge that would be very valuable in the future. After two years in that position, he took advantage of an opportunity to become a technical products buyer for a large municipal school district. For more than four years he was involved with buying computer systems and gained considerable experience in writing technical specifications and proposals. A year ago he moved to the banking industry and, because of his knowledge of computerized systems and supply requirements, was placed in charge of purchasing operational products and supervising a senior buyer and a buyer.

In his opinion, the most valuable part of his previous experience was in retail management because he gained a thorough understanding of business organization and procedures, a knowledge that is essential when buying the forms that drive the communications systems between the many departments of a full-service bank.

His experience in technical specification and proposal writing has also been very valuable because he has learned the art of organizing business communications in a clear and logical format.

According to Held, the ideal combination of education, skills, and experience for someone in his position would be a degree in a business-related field; highly developed skills in management, public, and interpersonal relations; a math background that would foster analytical abilities; and enough business experience to fully understand the broad picture of business operations.

Held also lists four critical needs for an effective purchasing official in the banking industry:

1. Must have excellent communication and negotiating skills.
2. Must establish goals, a practice heavily emphasized in the banking industry.
3. Must be service oriented. It is very important to deliver the right product to the user.
4. Must have a highly developed sense of ethical behavior and unquestionable integrity.

MERCHANDISING MANAGER
FOR A WHOLESALE GROCERY

Ray Gunther, an eighteen-year veteran in the purchasing field, is an excellent example of a professional who has succeeded in one of the most hectic of all types of buying—the perishable foods arena.

Working part time as a grocery clerk while finishing his formal schooling, Gunther decided to stay in retailing and started as an assistant grocery store manager. He soon was promoted to manager and then joined a large grocery chain as a pricing coordinator. His next move was to the warehousing and distribution function, and he was soon placed in a training program for grocery buyers. His next promotion was to director of grocery merchandising and then to vice-president of merchandising. Four years ago, he joined his present company as corporate manager of dairy merchandising and was then promoted to general merchandising manager. Currently, he supervises seven grocery buyers, five meat buyers, one dairy buyer, two frozen food buyers, five produce buyers, four people in the advertising department, and twelve print shop employees.

Gunther has a bachelor's degree in economics, but his formal education has been supplemented by countless training courses and seminars, including the three weeks' training per year sponsored by his company. When asked what part of his education has been most valuable in his career, Gunther identified math and computer science as having the greatest influence.

In terms of valuable work experience, he also thought that his involvement with the retail end of the grocery business gave him valuable insight into marketing practices. Since consumer perceptions and demands drive the retail business, this experience enables Gunther to help the retailers in merchandising the products.

Gunther also believes that an effective buyer in his area must have extensive product knowledge, information that cannot be learned in school; therefore, new employees are hired on the premise that they will possess the foundation or the capacity to become effective buyers. That necessary foundation, in Gunther's opinion, is a bachelor's degree in business or marketing and at least one year's experience in retailing or selling to retailers.

The newly hired buyer trainee is assigned to a division team and begins an intensive on-the-job training program. During the training, the newly hired employees are also evaluated in terms of certain characteristics that Gunther feels are necessary to be effective buyers in this industry. Ultimately, Gunther is looking for someone who is self-confident and amiable but demanding. This person also must have a very high level of integrity and professionalism and maintain an excellent business appearance.

All buyers are expected to be quality conscious and use the end-value approach to their purchasing activities. Since the food product marketplace is so unstable and unpredictable, attention must be constantly given to such factors as weather conditions, strikes, transportation problems, and any other factors that may affect the supply and demand cycle.

ASSISTANT MATERIALS MANAGER
IN MEDICAL SERVICES

After one year of college, family circumstances forced assistant materials manager Jay Selby to disrupt his formal education. His first position was in a hospital store as a store clerk. He was promoted to store manager, then assistant purchasing agent, and then to purchasing agent within a five-year period of time. He then accepted a senior buyer position in another hospital before moving to his present position in a large hospital located in a southwestern U.S. city.

Selby reports directly to the head of purchasing of a hospital with several operating locations. His responsibilities include the procurement of all support materials, equipment, and furniture for all locations with the exception of pharmaceuticals and dietary. Under the present system, these two departments order directly from the suppliers.

The requirements of a full-service hospital are so diverse and so specialized that Selby utilizes product evaluation committees to critique many of the products and equipment being considered for use. Each committee has a member of the materials management staff as an advisor to ensure that purchasing policy and standards are applied in each evaluation. These committees and medical staff specialists also assist in the writing of specifications and proposals particularly for highly complex medical equipment.

Continuous cooperation with the medical and technical departments is critical because much of the equipment and materials are used in life or death situations. In Selby's opinion, a hospital purchasing agent must have extensive product knowledge; however, because of the constant evolution of the medical field, only close cooperation with the technical departments can ensure that the proper products are procured.

The ideal educational background for a successful purchasing agent in the medical field is at least a bachelor's degree in a business-related major; however, there is no substitute for experience. As in many other fields, product knowledge can only be gained through experience on the job. Although Selby's experience may be supplemented by the numerous seminars and workshops that he attends, most of his knowledge is gained from the day-by-day contacts with the using departments and the product salespeople.

According to Selby, purchasing agents in the medical services area must be highly structured and mission oriented. The ability to be a team player is critical because of the very nature of the medical profession. It is a stressful profession because the allowance or the margin for error is so slight. The availability of the right product or equipment at the right time can be the difference between a person's life or death.

Selby also notes that there is an unusually high requirement for confidentiality. Consequently, a strong sense of ethics is mandatory.

MANAGER PURCHASING/MATERIALS CONTROL IN UTILITIES

After graduating from college with a BA in marketing, James Chapman, Jr., entered a management training program with a national department store chain and, within a year, became a department manager. Retailing, however, was not as attractive a field as he had anticipated, so, seeking a change, he accepted a position as an expediter with the local utilities company. Approximately 80 percent of his time was spent following up orders and checking the status of deliveries, which gave him the opportunity to gain considerable insight into the general gas and electric marketplace. He soon was promoted to a buyer position, and within a few years, he became a purchasing supervisor, which involved about 50 percent buying and 50 percent supervising other buyers. The utility company was expanding rapidly, and Chapman had the opportunity to become involved in the procurement of a wide range of products including office supplies, equipment, wire and cable, piping, steel, substation supplies, and communications equipment. The growth of the company provided an excellent training ground, and Chapman soon became familiar with most aspects of operating a utility company.

In 1982, he had the opportunity to join a utility company in a neighboring city as manager of purchasing. Soon after accepting the new position, he established a new code of ethics and developed a program of standard purchasing procedures. He also established a new traffic program directly linked to the expediting department. Several other departments were then placed under his supervision, including inventory control, reclamation of hazardous waste, and obsolete equipment disposal. Current plans call for the further addition of an inventory audit department and three systems analysts to aid in program development.

Currently he directs a staff of twenty in procurement, five in reclamation, ten in inventory control, and five in traffic/expediting. His purchasing volume will probably exceed 250 million dollars during 1989, and sales of obsolete equipment will top three million dollars.

Chapman described the best educational and experience background for someone in his position:

> Certainly a college degree, and I found a major in marketing to be very useful. I would also strongly recommend an MBA. A certified purchasing management designation should also be required. As far as experience is concerned, I would recommend ten to twelve years of purchasing and inventory control and considerable involvement with technical and legal issues. An individual should certainly have enough product knowledge to be able to make valid judg-

ments, but most utilities have engineering departments that develop specifications and proposals. You do need a working knowledge of the products to be able to communicate with other departments and the suppliers.

Chapman then added his opinion of an effective purchasing professional in his industry:

Utilities is a demanding environment. The pro has to juggle a number of projects at the same time, constantly reprioritizing. It is more of a fast-paced production function than most people think it is. The job requires a good analytical mind—the person must be self-starting and self-motivated, reasonably extroverted, and scenario oriented. By scenario oriented I mean that the person must be able to conceptualize the impact of several what-if situations before making a final judgment. They cannot be myopic or tunnel visioned. The utility industry survives on strategic long-term planning to cope with growth, and the pro has to learn to think the same way.

PROCUREMENT SPECIALIST IN ELECTRONICS

Steve Pottinger has an unusual alternative to consider when he investigates sources for electronic components. His company, a well-known semiconductor plant, has the capacity to manufacture many of the basic items needed. Consequently, many of his decisions are not where to buy but whether to make or buy. As a procurement specialist, he is constantly interacting with management in the development of potential foreign or offshore sources of contract manufacturing. He is also a member of several teams and committees including the implementation task force, various cost reduction teams, and the committee on operating policy and procedures.

Although he has been in purchasing for seventeen years, Pottinger started out as a computer operator, a job he held for three years. He then became a computer programmer and a software analyst. His introduction to the purchasing field occurred when he became an expediter and contract administrator for the same company. After a move to the western part of the country, he joined the buying staff of an international truck rental company and soon progressed to senior buyer and then to purchasing manager. His next position was purchasing manager for a commercial banking system. With a broad background in purchasing, he decided to become a consultant and set up the entire materials management system for an aircraft manufacturer in the process of relocating its primary manufacturing facility. Upon the completion of that project, he joined his current employer.

Pottinger has a bachelor's degree in materials management and is planning to go for his MBA. Because he uses so many different methods in procuring the products required by the company, he feels that the most essential knowledge involves the various purchasing systems and the administration of manufacturing contracts. Some product knowledge is necessary to know what questions to ask; however, most of the specifications are developed by engineering or by the customer.

He has found his computer background and experience to be very valuable, and obviously, some knowledge of contract law is essential. However, equally important is the development of the proper instincts and attitudes, attributes that are essential when interacting with management, suppliers, or customers.

When asked what the ideal educational background would be for someone wanting to enter his field, Pottinger replied: "The ideal combination would be engineering, communications, and law, a difficult combination to find under our current educational system. There is a strong technical orientation in our business, and we must depend upon teamwork and good communications to operate effectively."

DIRECTOR, CENTRAL PURCHASING
AGENCY IN EDUCATION

Mary Silva is another example of someone who entered the purchasing field through the back door. Upon graduating with a bachelor's degree in industrial psychology in the fifties, Silva accepted a position as business advisor to fraternities, sororities, and other student groups at a major eastern university. As the number of student organizations increased, it became obvious that the groups could save considerable money by centralizing their food, equipment, and other purchases. Consequently, Silva set up a system by which all of the purchases could be consolidated and yet delivery would still be made to each of the dozen organizations that were part of the original group. The system seemed simple—orders were collected and then placed with the supplier with the lowest price. When Silva received phone calls from a dozen irate chef–managers within thirty minutes after the first deliveries, she then decided that, in this field of purchasing, product knowledge was essential regardless of what system was used. She thus began a five-year process of self-education. A test kitchen was established and products were evaluated by a committee of cooks and managers. Specifications for major equipment were reviewed by engineering and service personnel, and quality standards for other products were established with the help of other university departments. She visited process plants and equipment manufacturing facilities and even helped break down sides of beef before she felt that she knew enough about the thousands of products purchased each year to be an effective buyer.

As the number of organizations participating in the centralized purchasing program approached sixty, Silva developed a central warehousing and distribution program that reduced the cost of nonperishables and equipment items.

Ultimately, the centralized concept was expanded to include accounting, personnel, maintenance, working capital investments, employee benefits, and insurance and accounts receivable/payable. Although she delegated the purchasing responsibility to a purchasing manager and staff, Silva retained a continued interest in the field.

When asked to describe the traits and knowledge necessary to be successful in her field, she replied:

> First, curiosity—you never can assume that you know all there is to know. Products and services evolve continuously, and you must remain up-to-date. Second, research and follow-through. You may know the product, but you also must know its use and the conditions of its use. For example, if a piece of equipment is intended to last fifteen years and it only lasts five, then we have erred someplace, either in our original specifications or in our projections as to the conditions of use. Third, the ability to analyze in terms of both concepts and mechanical relationships. Is a certain product the best for the intended use? Fourth, the ability to communicate, negotiate, and resolve conflict. Many times you are the link between the supplier and the user. It's a position that you cannot and should not avoid, but it requires tact, patience, understanding, and objectivity.

In Silva's opinion, the best possible combination of education and experience would be at least a bachelor's-level degree, preferably in materials management but including business law and three to five years' experience as an assistant buyer.

MANAGER OF PURCHASING IN MANUFACTURING

A twenty-seven-year veteran in the purchasing field, Robert Lutz is one of the few purchasing professionals interviewed who has been in the field since the beginning of his career. After college he entered the United States Air Force officer training school and, upon receiving his commission, was assigned to the aero-space program as a contract negotiator. His job involved the nego-tiations for research and development contracts for the Gemini program and also involved research on the space backpack project. Since contracting for research and development is limited almost entirely to government procurement, this experience pro-vided a unique approach to the skill or art of negotiating and prob-ably was responsible for his decision to stay in the purchasing field after he was discharged from the service.

His first civilian position was as a junior buyer, purchasing electronic components and fabricated parts. He then accepted a position as manager of purchasing and production with a hydrau-lic press manufacturer, a position he held for five years. He moved on to two purchasing manager positions in progressively larger companies before joining his present company as purchasing manager in 1982.

In his present position he supervises three buyers and three cler-ical personnel and directs the purchasing activities of one of the branches of a major company involved in the manufacture of a diverse range of products. Each of his buyers specializes in a spe-cific category of parts and materials, and although product knowl-edge is important, the knowledge of purchasing systems and organizational structure is critical because of the size of the plant and the relationships with other branches of the company.

As in most large basic manufacturing companies, the specifica-tions are developed in engineering and then, in cooperation with purchasing, are translated into purchase requisitions and orders. The buyers then begin the negotiations necessary to obtain the best products and the right price at the right time.

Lutz's primary responsibilities involve the constant review of corporate purchasing policies, needs assessments, staff training, systems design, and planning, which includes expediting, cost reporting and quality assurance, supplier/vendor evaluation, and cost/value analysis.

His educational background includes a bachelor of science degree, graduate-level courses, and numerous seminars sponsored by the National Association of Purchasing Management. Although his major was marketing, he feels that the basic business courses were the most help in his career. He also feels that the negotiating experience gained in the air force plus his independent studies in negotiating have been extremely valuable.

According to Lutz, the ideal combination of education and experience for someone managing the purchasing function in a manufacturing environment is a bachelor's degree in business with a concentration in materials management and a diverse working background that should include both large- and small-company experience. Working for a small company gives a person the opportunity to become familiar with all aspects of company operations, and large-company experience provides a more specialized training in formal purchasing systems.

An ideal character and attitude profile could be described as inquisitive, outgoing, well organized, good written and oral communications skills, and, above all, good listening skills, since much essential information is obtained from sales personnel.

Lutz also mentioned that there were three little-known requirements for success in the purchasing field: first, the need to take action—that is, the need to continuously seek out alternatives or options, never being satisfied that the current method is the only method; second, understanding the value of the function of purchasing in the organizational structure; third, the ability to negotiate win–win contracts with suppliers.

At this point in his career, Lutz is not looking at his position as a stepping-stone to a general management position. His real expertise lies in purchasing, and he is totally committed to the field as a lifetime career.

DIRECTOR OF PURCHASING
FOR THE GOVERNMENT

Sandy Spain is the director of purchasing for a southwestern U.S. city internationally known as a tourist mecca. Although she has been in purchasing only five years, she has much experience in government operations, particularly in the financial sector. Her first significant government position was as a planning and zoning administrator. After approximately ten years in that position, she became manager of customer services, a job involving the billing and collection of utilities, sales, and business taxes. Her next move was to the position of assistant to the city treasurer, where she was heavily involved in numerous financial projects. In 1984, she was asked to take the position of director of purchasing for the city. Her primary qualification for the position was her in-depth knowledge of how government really works and her service-oriented attitude. She fully understands that the taxpayers are the source of the funds that she spends and the purchasing systems must be designed to protect their rights.

Currently her responsibilities include the direction of thirty-one employees in purchasing, central receiving and stores, inventory control, printing and binding, and the mail room. She also is in charge of a portion of accounts payable since her department processes all of the invoices and statements for payment by central accounting. Her purchasing department is segmented in three phases: purchasing administration, bid and contract specialists, and buyers of products and services (under bid limits).

As in most government buying agencies, Spain's purchasing methods are highly visible and public. Many of her suppliers are also taxpayers, and therefore, her purchasing systems must be open and fair to all who wish to sell to the city. All purchases above a predetermined dollar limit are made according to formal bidding procedures, with the exception of those products obtained through a cooperative purchasing agreement with the state. Formal bidding procedures require that the development of specifications be an exacting process and, again, must be designed to allow a variety of suppliers to submit bids.

Vendor evaluation is an important function of her department and is done through a combination of customer feedback and a computer program that tracks delivery and quality performance. She also meets regularly with the various city departments to critique both her department's performance and the supplier of both products and services.

Spain's educational background includes two years of college and numerous seminars on government operations and purchasing. Although she feels that a four-year degree in business would provide a good basic foundation, she does believe that a concentration in purchasing would not be as valuable in government as it might be in other applications because most schools tend to lean toward manufacturing as a basis for teaching purchasing techniques. Government purchasing requires considerable product knowledge usually obtained by experience, but unlike the private sector, there is the additional requirement of knowing formal bidding systems and how to effectively build positive relationships with both the citizens and the suppliers.

According to Spain, one of the most interesting aspects of municipal purchasing is the variety of products and services. Almost every day brings a different challenge, particularly when a product or service must be customized to fill a unique need. Requirements range from building construction to pencils and from vehicles to mud pits for park activities, all requiring much coordination with other city departments.

Spain's example of an ideal government purchasing manager is someone who is analytical and customer-service oriented with excellent math and evaluation skills and thoroughly adept in the art of negotiating. Since this position is constantly under the scrutiny of the public, the highest ethical standards are a must. A government purchasing manager must also be detail minded and be able to operate effectively within a relatively rigid organizational structure.

Her considerable experience in working within a government structure has given her a thorough understanding of what the city demands of her department. She is, at this point, considering making purchasing management a career.

RETAIL DIVISIONAL MERCHANDISING MANAGER

As divisional merchandising manager, Steven Dye supervises four buyers and four assistant buyers in the textile division of a major nationwide department store chain. His primary responsibility involves bath, bedding, and curtain and drapery products. Also, unlike managers in most textile departments, he is responsible for buying lamp and luggage products. A veteran of fifteen years in purchasing, most of his experience has been in retail sales and merchandising. After graduating from college with a degree in marketing, he entered a training program with another major chain and has had a series of positions including assistant sales manager, assistant buyer, buyer, assistant store manager, and regional merchandising manager at the corporate level.

As in most large retailing chains, the training program and the executive development track have exposed him to both sides of department store operations—sales and merchandising—giving him the broad overview of retailing. The opportunity to experience all aspects of operations has enabled Dye to function as a member of a complex, fast-paced system of buying and marketing consumer products. He and his team are responsible for the selection, procurement, and merchandising of a broad range of products that appeal to both the high and low end of the markets.

Dye's buyers must be very sensitive to consumer preferences and trends because they must determine the market, shop the sources, price the products, and then promote them. Understandably, they are very brand conscious because most retailers will identify with certain labels or manufacturers that, in turn, are targeted toward the upper or lower price markets.

Usually Dye uses an open-end contract to buy most of the products. The various branches are then supplied with their needs at a price guaranteed for the length of the contract, which is usually written for a specific period of time or for the season. Since each division will buy for stores in several states, the buyers must also accommodate customer needs under a variety of climatic conditions and local trends.

Dye has found his background in all aspects of store operations to be most valuable in his career. Although he now has obtained his MBA, he feels that it is most important to be multidisciplined and to pay particular attention to the basics of retailing. The knowledge gained during his MBA program has been very valuable in the strategic planning aspects of his current position.

Extensive product knowledge is also a must in department store operations since buying for multilevel price markets requires an acute sense of perceived value and cost. The buyers are constantly making rapid value comparison judgments.

The best background for someone entering this field is a four-year degree in business and marketing, demonstrated achievement in a related field, and some type of retail or customer service experience.

As far as character and personality traits are concerned, Dye describes the ideal retailing professional as emotionally stable, realistic, a good listener, even tempered, self-disciplined, self-motivated, and having common sense.

DIRECTOR OF CONTRACTING
IN MANUFACTURING

John Mihelich is a classic example of someone who made it to the executive level the hard way. He started working in the sheet metal shop of a major aircraft and aerospace manufacturer and then spent time in the machine shop, in processing, and then in warehousing as an expediter. During this time, he was attending college at night and received his BS degree and his MBA. His career began to materialize, and he progressed rapidly through a series of positions involving the administration of programs and projects relating to the space shuttle and the B1B bomber. Some of his job titles were senior operations administrator, program/project management representative, senior major subcontract administrator, section manager—material, group manager—material. Most of these positions involved the subcontracting for aircraft systems and complex electromechanical equipment. Three years ago he accepted a position with a telecommunications company as director of contracting.

His current duties involve the development of contracts for all the products required by the company with an annual purchasing volume in excess of one billion dollars.

At this point, he is returning to his former employer after accepting a position as purchasing manager with the opportunity to manage the entire materials organization.

During most of his career, he has been involved in contract administration, positions that require highly developed negotiating skills and a level of product knowledge that enable him to understand and communicate basic configurations and to negotiate contract modifications and changes. He has found that his manufacturing and shop experience has given him a sense of quality values and an understanding of the critical nature of timing that has been a great help in his career. He also feels that his involvement in the

MBA program gave him the opportunity to learn from facilitators who actually work in related industries, again providing him with a better overview of operations.

In his opinion, the best educational and experience background for someone in his position is a BS degree, eventually an MBA, and experience in manufacturing, project and program management, and a solid background in negotiating. The person also must be consistent, a hard driver, fair in pursuing win–win relationships both internally and externally, and a good planner, implementer, and motivator. Procurement personnel in manufacturing must be multifaceted with knowledge of engineering, quality control, production/operations, and price analysis.

CHAPTER 6

PURCHASING IN THE
COMPUTER/ELECTRONICS INDUSTRY

THE NATURE OF THE WORK

The computer and electronics industry is unlike most of the other industries for two very important reasons. First, most of its competition is foreign; this complicates the needs assessment process and the competitive cost process in product development. Second, this industry is one of the few that often has the capability of manufacturing many of the components that it requires. Consequently, the decision to make or buy must be made early in the procurement process, and the necessity to project production costs adds another challenging dimension to the purchasing department's responsibilities.

Another complicating factor, although not unique to the computer/electronics industry, is that many of the parts, components, and materials are purchased from foreign, or offshore, sources. This means that an already very complicated procurement process is further complicated by differences in time, language, and international law. Since this industry, as all others, is concerned with the cost of materials management, the need for timely deliveries is extremely important; this also is often complicated by transportation or shipping problems due to distance and the need to use a variety of transportation methods in obtaining each product. The variety of transportation can also make the expediter's job a nightmare when he or she is trying to determine the status of a shipment.

The emphasis in the purchasing system in a computer/electronics environment is on the ability to negotiate. Although some product knowledge is useful in knowing the right questions to ask, realistically it would be impossible to know everything about every product or component involved. Specifications are usually developed by engineering or, more often, the customer. Military and international markets are primary customers, and these users usually have very exacting specifications and requirements. Exceptions to this rule are those manufacturers producing consumer products; however, their numbers have fallen due to foreign competition.

Purchasing professionals in this industry spend much of their time in meetings with management and other departments. The need to coordinate all of the company's primary activities almost always involves purchasing because of its input regarding costs, availability, and sources. The ability to relate to top management, other departments, and suppliers, sometimes foreign, is absolutely essential. Buying decisions are not as much a matter of numbers as in some industries simply because of the intangibles: timing, reliability of contractors, communications, and international politics.

ENTRY REQUIREMENTS AND QUALIFICATIONS

Entry into the computer/electronics field is usually gained through expediting or buyer trainee positions, although some buyers enter through complex clerical or computer programming jobs. Technical or computer experience is very helpful in finding that first job because in most cases you will be working in a highly complex manufacturing environment. The ideal educational background is a degree in engineering with heavy emphasis in business and business law or a degree in business with emphasis in business or international law. Work experience should include some computer or electronic applications because familiarity with the basic technical concepts is required. Also important is a demonstrated ability to work with various levels of people in a business/technical relationship.

Although some specific product knowledge is helpful, the true expertise required is in the procurement systems themselves. There is a divided opinion concerning the value of a college major in materials management. Some feel that companies' systems are so specialized, applying to only one segment of the computer/electronics industry, that a person can learn them only through on-the-job training. Others, however, are of the opinion that formal coursework, particularly at the graduate level, significantly increases advancement potential. One person noted that the formal courses in the PTO (purchasing, transportation, and operations) major gave him a better understanding of some of the options available when designing or administrating procurement systems.

This industry will have high expectations for you. In addition to technical expertise and the knowledge of procurement procedures, the industry wants excellent negotiating skills and instincts. Since this industry depends on operating committees and task forces for many of its policies and procedures, the ability to work as part of several teams concurrently is important. The fact that many products are manufactured according to customer specifications results in the need to interact with sales and the actual customers perhaps more than in most other industries.

Most purchasing professionals working in this field stress the need for employees who are detail oriented, patient, not easily frustrated, excellent problem solvers, skilled in written and verbal communications, and well organized. In certain segments of this industry, a fluency in a second language is also a definite plus. Obviously, the knowledge of Chinese or Japanese would be very useful, and because of increasing activity in Mexico, fluency in Spanish is also desirable.

WORKING CONDITIONS

You can expect above-average starting salaries and good fringe benefit packages. The working environment is usually excellent, with modern facilities. The work group is comprised of technically oriented professionals, and you will spend much of your time interacting with various departments and management. The pace is sometimes hectic, and when problems do occur, they tend to be complex simply because the procurement systems are complex.

CHAPTER 7

PURCHASING IN THE WHOLESALE/RETAIL INDUSTRY

The wholesale/retail classification of purchasing systems includes department stores, food stores, supermarkets, and chain specialty shops. Although small independent shops also have to buy their merchandise, usually the buying is one of the responsibilities of owners or managers, but only a part of their daily activities. Since you are primarily interested in purchasing as a career, only the larger chains or franchises will be covered in this chapter.

The wholesale/retail business has been in a period of transition during the past two or three decades as the number of large independent operations has virtually disappeared. In their place, a limited number of giant wholesalers and retailers with sometimes hundreds of branch operations has emerged. General merchandise wholesalers have also been declining in numbers as retailing chains have grown so much that they are able to eliminate the wholesaler and buy directly from the manufacturer because of the enormous volume they purchase. The food wholesaler, however, still commands a sizable portion of the nation's business because large supermarket chains find buying directly from food producers and manufacturers to be impractical in many cases, especially because much of their merchandise is perishable. Because of the current trends in wholesaling and retailing, career paths will be outlined in four major areas: department stores, food chains at the retail level, food wholesaling, and chain specialty shops.

DEPARTMENT STORES

The Nature of the Work

Currently, most department store chains have two principal operating functions: merchandising, and store organization and sales. The merchandising side is responsible for selecting products, buying products, pricing, marketing strategies, and advertising. The sales side is principally involved with sales personnel, training, and store operations. Product lines are split into three broad categories: women's, which may include cosmetics, perfumes, accessories, clothing and sportswear, juniors, and intimate apparel; men's, which may include tailored clothing and accessories, sportswear, and children's clothing and accessories; and housewares, which includes tabletop, textiles (bath and bed), and small wares (such as lamps and luggage). The responsibility for buying and marketing these products is usually split among eight to twelve division merchandise managers, and each manager will have from three to ten buyers. The buyers specialize in certain types of products. For example, one buyer may handle towels and bed items; another, men's sportswear; and another, table lamps.

Retail buyers are unique among purchasing professionals. While buyers in other industries respond to the needs of other departments by buying what they have requested, retail buyers actually choose what they will buy, price it, and market it. Unlike most other purchasing professionals, retail buyers are very brand conscious because stores carry certain lines of merchandise, particularly in clothing, cosmetics, perfumes, and accessories. Since they are responsible for the selection of the products to be sold, retail buyers are very sensitive to market trends and current fads, a responsibility normally belonging to sales or product development. Most product lines that carry a brand name are quite extensive, and the buyer must know enough about his or her particular market to select those items that will sell.

Generally, retail buyers use an open-end quotation, meaning that the prices quoted will be good for the season or for a specific period of time. Branch stores may either reorder against the season contract or, if the retailer has a regional warehousing and distribution center, from the regional headquarters. Many stores have point-of-sale computer equipment, and often purchase orders against existing contracts are computer generated and do not involve the buyer.

Entry Requirements and Qualifications

Entry into a retail buying career is usually through a buyer training program. Approximately 80 to 85 percent of those entering the training program are recruited from colleges, and the remaining 15 to 20 percent are recruited from within the company. About 85 percent of the buyers come from this training, and 15 percent are lateral transfers. Training programs are usually well structured. After a period of classroom and on-the-job training, the candidates are then placed as assistant sales personnel or assistant buyers. After one year, the candidate then switches to the other side, so that each candidate has the chance to experience both sales and merchandising.

Some travel is required, particularly in the clothing and fashion areas, and surveying the market and consumer trends is a constant part of the job. Most companies encourage continuing education through seminars and workshops centering around product knowledge and marketing.

Retailing is driven by product knowledge and marketing with relatively little emphasis on systems. Buyers must have a well-developed sense of product value because often they are buying both the low and high end of the same product and must balance the pricing between the cost and the competition. Generally, those seeking success in retail buying must be self-motivated, self-disciplined, realistic with much common sense, even tempered, creative, and imaginative. Their work will be the subject of considerable sales dialogue, so they must be good listeners with analytical minds.

Working Conditions

Beginning salaries are competitive, particularly through the college recruiting programs, and fringe benefits are above average. Working conditions are usually excellent, with state-of-the-art equipment. The pace is fast but organized, and the atmosphere is professional. Advancement opportunities are very good and often involve a change in location.

RETAIL FOOD/SUPERMARKET

The term *supermarket* has been included as a type of retail food market, even though there is a pronounced trend toward expanding the product lines to include housewares, clothing, textiles, cameras, and music. Some stores now devote over half of their floor space to nonfood items. Other changes over the past three decades have drastically changed the nature of the retail buyer's responsibilities. The most significant changes have been: first, the almost complete transition from butchering at the store level to buying boxed or Cryovac fresh meats in which most of the breakdown of the carcasses is done at the processing plants; second, the expanded use of prepacks; and, third, the expansion of the precooked frozen lines. Most of these changes have made the life of the retail buyer much easier, since the packers have assumed some of the responsibility for quality control. Some of the changes, however, have reduced retail buyers' ability to buy effectively because quality cannot be determined until the package or the box is actually opened. They now must depend more on random sampling, which, in the food business, is less effective than most other products.

The Nature of the Work

Most food/supermarket chains are organized on a regional basis. There may be one corporate headquarters, but the marketing territories are broken up into regions. Each region has a staff of buyers, particularly for perishable items, and also usually has a warehousing and distribution center. Often contracts for brand-name standard items and branded nonfood items are negotiated at corporate level, so there are opportunities for purchasing careers at both the regional and national headquarter levels.

In most regional purchasing departments, buying functions are separated into two major divisions: food and general merchandise. Each of these divisions is then further separated according to product categories, such as fresh fruits and vegetables, meats, dairy, cheeses, frozen foods, canned items, and bakery and specialties. In general merchandise, they are broken down into clothing, bed and bath, and housewares. As in the department store field, buyers are responsible for product selection and pricing.

Perhaps in no other segment of the purchasing field is product knowledge so important as in the buying of foods, because most foods are not manufactured and the quality and supply is subject to the whims of nature and the processors. A food buyer cannot inspect a carload of lettuce and expect that every carload he or she receives from that particular grower is going to be equal in quality for the next six months. Most assuredly the quality will not be the same. Weather conditions change, harvesting may be too early or too late, transportation can be delayed—all factors that affect the quality and condition of the products. Consequently, continuous sampling and inspection, especially when buying the fresh perishable products, is a standard part of the purchasing department's procedure.

Most of the products in the processed foods and general merchandise lines are national brands, and in many chains, master contracts for branded products are negotiated at corporate level. There are, however, many products that are in demand and available only on a regional level, and the regional buyers have the authority to stock those items. This fact emphasizes another unique characteristic of retail buyers. They must know both ends of the market—they must know the market conditions surrounding the source of the products, and they must also be sensitive to the demands of the consumer.

Working Conditions

The working environment is usually in a typical office building, not a store, since, as noted before, most buying functions take place at the regional or corporate level. The equipment is updated, and the systems are highly computerized. Point-of-sale-based systems provide a database that is extremely helpful and effective in tracking consumer trends.

Because the timing of deliveries is so important and there are so many uncontrollable factors involved, the work pace is sometimes very fast and stressful. An average supermarket carries twelve to sixteen thousand different items, and stores with large general merchandise sections carry in excess of twenty thousand items—both tremendous volumes. Buyers must be highly organized and yet flexible enough to cope with the many minor problems that surface daily.

Since each buyer has his or her product niche, there is much autonomy in the purchasing department. Therefore, buyers must be self-disciplined and able to work effectively without close supervision. Since second guessing the markets is so much a part of their daily routine, an analytical mind and the ability to grasp complex data quickly is essential. It is interesting to note, however, that among all the professionals interviewed for this book, buyers in this category most often described their jobs as exciting.

Entry Requirements

Entry-level positions are more often found in the sales area than in department store chains. Produce buyers, meat buyers, and others often come up from the store levels where they were involved in the sale and display of the products. Most of the chains also recruit from college campuses and have formal buyer training programs very similar to department stores.

Salaries and Benefits

Salaries are average to slightly below average at the entry level, but senior buyers and above receive very nice compensation packages that include substantial fringe benefits. Retailing is a relatively high turnover industry; therefore, advancement is quite rapid. As in any chain operation, promotion usually requires relocation.

WHOLESALE FOOD

The Nature of the Work

The wholesaling of food products is a complex area simply because of the variety of products and the number of different markets served. First, the prime markets of the wholesaler are separated into two very distinct categories: institutions/restaurants/hotels and retail. Each category requires different packaging of the products, and in some cases, the products may be processed or prepared in a completely different way for each market. The wholesalers themselves may specialize, some according to products, such as meat, fish, or produce, and others by market, such as the HRI (hotel, restaurant, and institutional) supplier. The trend, however, is toward multimarket and multiproduct line operations and, as in the retail arena, toward nationwide companies with regional semiautonomous branches. This trend is opening up excellent opportunities for skilled purchasing professionals in an obviously essential industry.

It is at the wholesale level that the buyer's job takes on another dimension, that of buying for private labels. Every wholesaler carries the national brands, such as Campbell's, Kraft, and Hunt's. In addition to these national brands, many wholesalers carry a duplicate line of products under their own private label, usually priced 5 to 15 percent less than the national brands. These private label items are bought from various packers who specialize in processing for both private label and national brands. The quality of the products of the packers and processors varies considerably, and it is the job of the buyer to choose that proper balance between price and quality that will appeal to the lower end of the consumer market. The choice is made by a procedure known as blind cutting. Each potential supplier, packer, and processor is invited to submit a sample of a product. The label is stripped from each sample and the container is coded so that the samplers will not know who packed or processed the product. The samples are graded for taste, texture, color, and fill by the buyers, who will try to find the right price–quality balance. Grading these samples requires an exceptional amount of product knowledge that sometimes takes years to accumulate.

In addition to their own private labels, some wholesalers also enter into relatively long-term contracts to supply retail chains or large independents with products under the retailer's label. It is the buyer's responsibility, again, to locate the best product for the price.

In practically every instance, product knowledge can only be gained through experience. Consequently, potential buyers will either be pulled from the retail ranks or be placed in an extensive buyer training program. Many are recruited from college campuses, although most larger companies prefer someone who has also had at least a year in retailing.

Although buyers must be sensitive to consumer trends, the heavy emphasis is on a thorough knowledge of the product markets and the conditions that could affect supply and quality. They must always be ready to find and use alternate sources of supply, particularly for perishable items.

Entry Requirements and Qualifications

Some familiarity with computer systems is helpful for potential buyers since most modern wholesalers track inventory levels and reorder points through data processing. As noted before, many buyer trainees are obtained through college recruitment programs, although at least a year's experience in retailing is preferred. Buyer trainees are also recruited from the retail levels, particularly from the dairy, produce, and meat departments.

Those hiring potential buyers look for someone who is self-confident; amiable, but capable of being firm and demanding; and in control at all times, remaining calm under circumstances that are beyond his or her control. A professional appearance and a high level of integrity are also very important. Those who prefer a high level of activity and variety will find this field very satisfying.

Working Conditions

Working conditions are similar to those in retailing, and the salary and fringe benefit levels are also similar. For some reason, turnover is less in wholesaling, and the consolidation trends seem to provide more than adequate advancement opportunities. At times the pace is extremely fast, and the wholesale buyer is also often subject to the whims of nature.

CHAIN OR FRANCHISE SPECIALTY STORES

The Nature of the Work

Although buying positions in specialty retailing and wholesaling are very similar to those in similar supermarket and department areas, there are some significant differences. First, specialty shops are more apt to deal exclusively with imported products, which makes finding adequate sources and then negotiating favorable transportation more complicated. Second, product knowledge and an extensive knowledge of the marketplace is absolutely critical. Third, buyers in specialty areas travel more than their counterparts in other types of retailing.

Entry Requirements

Because of the extensive product and market knowledge requirements, entry into specialty buying is usually limited to those who have considerable experience in retailing or selling to retailers. Unless a prospective buyer has experience in the line of products featured by the specialty shops, he or she will still have to serve an apprenticeship before going out alone.

Salaries and Benefits

Salaries are usually higher than average, and working conditions range from good to superior. Specialty shop buyers must be self-motivated and disciplined since much of the time they work independently. They must have an acute sense of value/cost since most of the products they buy are known as high-ticket items. Specialty shops are not usually high-volume sellers and consequently depend on higher profit margins for survival. Mistakes in judging the market and the pricing levels can be costly; therefore, specialty buyers are greater risk takers than buyers in most other fields.

A CHALLENGING FIELD

At this point you have probably realized that the purchasing function in the wholesale/retail field has an added dimension to the responsibilities of being a buyer. Not only do buyers purchase the product to be sold, in many cases they also choose the products. Therefore, there is an unusual requirement to know consumer trends and markets. There is also the need to market to various levels, which means the buyer must know the low, medium, and high ends of consumer demand. Unlike most other industries, the buyer is also involved in the merchandising of the product, an area of responsibility usually reserved for sales.

This field of purchasing is demanding and fast paced; however, there are few fields more challenging and varied. If you like a challenge, a variety of responsibilities, and handling many projects at the same time, take a close look at this career field. It may offer many challenges, but it also offers many rewards.

CHAPTER 8

PURCHASING IN THE HOSPITALITY INDUSTRY

THE NATURE OF THE WORK

The hospitality industry serves a wide range of activities involving travel, entertainment, business, and recreation. Consequently, your place of business could be a hotel, restaurant, resort, conference center, motel, country club, or any other operation that caters to the public by offering food and lodging. You could work on site or in the corporate headquarters, since many in the hospitality industry are part of a chain or franchise operation.

Generally, the product classifications are food and beverage, janitorial and office supplies, furniture and equipment, recreational equipment, vehicles, landscape equipment, and supplies and services. Since many of the products are consumables, the volume and the delivery activity is extremely high.

Food Buyers

Perhaps the most complex field, the one requiring the most product knowledge, is the position of food buyer. The availability of the basic products, meats, poultry, fruits, vegetables, grains, spices, and seafood, depends upon the whims of nature, a force that cannot be controlled. Therefore, the food buyer must be in

93

constant contact with the markets to determine not only pricing and quality but also availability. When weather conditions sharply diminish supply they also significantly affect the quality of the items that are available. Consequently, the buyer must always be in a position to substitute items and to coordinate the substitution with all the users.

Almost every food product is available in various grades of quality. Beef, for example, is available in several grades that relate to tenderness and the method of cooking. There are also several yield grades that relate to cost. Knowing what quality grade and what yield grade to buy requires a thorough knowledge of beef and the many ways that it can be used. The same approach must also be used with pork, veal, poultry, seafood, and most fruits and vegetables, regardless of whether the item is purchased fresh, canned, or frozen.

This in-depth knowledge of food products can be gained only through extensive hands-on experience, a fact that favors the person who wishes to enter the purchasing field but does not have a degree. However, the lack of a degree may hamper him or her at the upper management levels. To make the jump from senior buyer to purchasing manager or director of purchasing may mean that the person will have to return to school to obtain some type of post-secondary education.

Purchasing foods in the private sector is usually based on an open market buying system—receiving quotations on prices from several vendors that have been selected because of their past history of quality and service. After receiving the quotations, often the purchasing agent will require that product samples be submitted for testing, particularly if the item is canned or packaged. In better hotels, resorts, and restaurants, the price is secondary to the quality because, obviously, the quality determines the overall image and reputation of the establishment.

Beverage Purchasing

Beverage purchasing, which includes wines and liquors, also requires extensive product knowledge. Again, the reputation of the establishment depends upon the ability of the buyer to select the best wines and liquors in every price range for a variety of uses. Often the selection of wines is based on the requirements of the wine steward, who is usually responsible for maintaining the wine cellar.

Buying Consumable Products

Most other consumable products, such as office and housekeeping supplies, recreational equipment, and landscaping products, are also purchased on the open market. Specifications for these products and supplies are developed in cooperation with the appropriate departments. Products in this category are not perishable and, therefore, are usually purchased in volume, stored, and then distributed as needed, a function normally under the direction of the purchasing department.

Buying Major Equipment and Furniture

In most chain or franchise operations, the purchase of major equipment and furniture, particularly in lobbies, lounges, and other common areas, is coordinated through purchasing or interior design departments at the regional or national corporate headquarters. Since most chains and franchises wish to maintain a certain theme or image, the furnishings, the colors, and the fixtures must be consistent from one location to another, thus requiring control by a corporate-level department. Even if the local buyer actually orders the items, the specifications are usually developed by corporate, or the items are purchased through contracts negotiated at the corporate level.

In many cases, the purchasing policies and procedures used by the local buyers are established by the corporate purchasing department, which may also negotiate nationwide contracts for some types of food, beverage, and supply products that are available through local distribution facilities. These contracts might involve national brand condiments, detergents, beverages, processed canned and frozen foods, or minor equipment.

Although corporate-level purchasing departments also require extensive product knowledge, they are more likely to require more formal education in business, interior design, engineering, and purchasing. Because they negotiate larger and longer-term contracts and because they must coordinate purchasing for many locations, there is a greater need for understanding overall corporate goals.

ENTRY REQUIREMENTS AND QUALIFICATIONS

Entry-level positions are varied. Since product knowledge is generally the essential requirement, many workers in hospitality purchasing started in apprentice-like positions in food and beverage service, housekeeping, or general clerical. Although increasingly a college degree is required, particularly at corporate levels, there are still many opportunities for high school graduates or two-year college graduates to enter the field, particularly if they have taken courses relating to the industry.

If you are considering a career in purchasing in the hospitality industry, then you must be aware of the demands placed on workers in this field. The hospitality field is driven by deadlines—orders must be in by a certain time and deliveries must be scheduled to coincide with guest arrivals, banquets, weddings, conferences, and other special events. Restaurants cannot accurately forecast volume or what the guests will order, so inventory levels must be adequate and flexible. Deliveries for events are often scheduled for the day of the event, so the time of delivery is critical. It is not unusual for a large resort to have three or four restaurants, several lounges, and five to ten banquet rooms capable of serving up to twelve hundred people. The demands will differ every day, and each day will bring different challenges and problems.

Consequently, if you are someone who must have an orderly and highly structured working environment, then this industry is not for you. This industry is for people who love high levels of activity, a variety of daily challenges, and interaction with many people. It is fast paced, hectic, exciting, and, for those who can cope with the pace, highly satisfying. No matter how organized you are, because the numbers and demand vary daily, your activities in the hospitality business can never be completely planned.

A sense of humor is vital. Daily you will be involved in tense situations where a sense of humor is a good method of relieving tension. The ability to work as a member of a team is also critical, because the need to coordinate many activities on a daily and even hourly basis is constant. You must be able to accept problem solving as a way of life and be even tempered. You must be highly adaptive and creative and be able to accept changes without reacting negatively.

A sense of fairness and the ability to establish long-term vendor relationships is important. It is not at all unusual for the hospitality buyer to ask vendors to make emergency deliveries because of last minute changes in banquet menus or other problems. However, vendors need to feel that they are not being taken advantage of.

A buyer in this industry has to be reasonably extroverted and assertive. Because of the high levels of activity, the buyer must have an air of authority and must control the pace. He or she must have the ability to interrelate with a wide range of personality types, including chefs and interior designers, corporate executives, and delivery people.

The ideal combination of education and experience for some-one wishing to enter hospitality purchasing is in the product information area. Since product information can only be obtained through hands-on experience, the "coming up through the ranks" approach as a source of purchasing personnel is the most common. In larger chains, a trend toward hiring people with an associate's or bachelor's degree in food service or hotel/motel administration is noticeable. However, those hired in this category usually enter extensive training or intern programs designed to provide the necessary product knowledge.

Those entering the field in the hands-on entry-level positions are well advised to take college-level courses in purchasing, management, and business administration in order to improve their potential for promotion. At some point in your career, you may have the opportunity to apply or qualify for a supervisory position. At that point, a more thorough knowledge of the principles of purchasing and management systems will help obtain that promotion.

CHAPTER 9

PURCHASING IN THE UTILITIES INDUSTRY

THE NATURE OF THE WORK

Work in the utilities industry can be either in the public or private sector. Although most utility companies are privately owned and operate on the basis of contractual agreements with the municipalities that they service, there are still many that are owned and operated by cities and, in a few instances, the federal government. Those in the private sector usually are controlled or monitored by some type of a government commission; however, the purchasing policies are determined by the company.

Purchasing departments in utility companies tend to have several operating subdepartments because they are involved in all aspects of the energy system. They manufacture the product, distribute it directly to the consumer, and service the distribution network. Meeting the demands of all of these functions involves the purchasing department in the procurement of a wide range of products and services. The range of products may be further complicated if the company is involved with all of the basic energy sources: electricity, gas, water, and nuclear.

The product classifications range from office supplies to complex nuclear equipment and include such specialized items as substation components, transmission equipment, and sophisticated computer and electronic control equipment.

Since purchasing may include expediting, traffic, service fleet management, inventory control, audit and systems analysis, surplus equipment disposal, and hazardous waste handling departments, there are numerous entry-level positions that can lead to buyer, senior buyer, department manager, or supervisor. The more obvious choices are expediting, inventory control, and systems analysis, and many of the companies have well-established buyer- and manager-training programs. A college degree is becoming necessary to progress into management-level positions, and the preferred major concentration is in business or marketing. At the higher levels, an MBA and designation as a certified purchasing manager is preferred.

Because of the variety of products and services purchased, almost all types of procurement systems are used: open market quote, price index, informal and formal bid, and negotiated short- and long-term or open-end contracts. Consequently, buyers must be familiar with most purchasing systems and techniques. Product knowledge requirements also vary since the engineering department usually develops the specifications for the more complicated technical equipment. Buyers also tend to be extremely quality oriented. Faulty or poor quality equipment results in interruptions of service, a situation that most utility companies try to avoid.

Utility companies in general are monopolies, a status that has the advantage of no competition but the disadvantage of being in the public eye. This high visibility creates considerable pressure, as the public becomes very vocal when service is poor. Sensitivity to public opinion is felt throughout the entire organization, and purchasing is no exception.

Most companies have been in business for a long time and, therefore, are well established and organized. The atmosphere is structured but not unreasonably so. Most purchasing professionals are very comfortable with the amount of flexibility and autonomy found in utilities, particularly in the private sector, because they can respond effectively to emergency situations without being bound by an overly rigid purchasing system.

ENTRY REQUIREMENTS AND QUALIFICATIONS

In terms of desired character traits, you are expected to be self-starting and self-motivated, confident and outgoing, strong under pressure, and even tempered under all types of circumstances. In this industry more than most, the ability to think in terms of scenarios is extremely important. Almost every decision must include alternatives or options. One purchasing professional calls these options fallback positions. Although many products are purchased through long-term open-end contracts, alternate sources of supply must always be available.

Most utility companies in the public sector operate under the same general guidelines. Because of their responsibilities in the event of an emergency, their purchasing systems are often independent of the government entity, at least in the area of specialized and emergency equipment. Employment selection and advancement is usually subject to civil service regulations. You should, at this point, be aware that these regulations may differ from one government entity to another, so each position that you consider has to be investigated as to the terms of employment.

The utility industry is very supportive of those employees who wish to supplement their education by taking regular college courses, seminars, and workshops. Executives are encouraged to become active in related trade and professional associations and community affairs. Many purchasing professionals belong to the local affiliates of the National Association of Purchasing Managers and actively involve themselves in the association's various committees. Considering their rather unique status as monopolies regulated by commissions or government agencies, it is easy to understand why utilities encourage employees at all levels to become involved in civic and charitable activities. All departments are expected to cooperate in maintaining excellent relations with the general public and the local municipal governments.

WORKING CONDITIONS

Compensation levels are average to above average with excellent fringe benefits. Employment is stable with above-average job security. The work environment is usually pleasant and the facilities well equipped. The work can be very fast paced, particularly during emergencies and adverse weather conditions when priorities are suddenly changed.

CHAPTER 10

PURCHASING IN MEDICAL SERVICES

The category of medical services includes hospitals, clinics, extended-care facilities, dental groups, and specialty institutions. Medical services also includes thousands of doctors' and dental offices too small to require a full-time purchasing agent or buyer. Therefore, we will discuss only the larger health-related organizations.

The field of medical services is separated into two distinct categories: the public sector, financed through tax dollars; and the private sector, financed through patient fees and charitable donations. Public and private sector purchasing systems have very significant differences and often require workers with different backgrounds and personality types.

PRIVATE MEDICAL SERVICES

The Nature of the Work

The purchasing department in a private institution is usually responsible to the chief financial or administrative officer, and unless the institution is part of a medical care system or chain, the departmental policies and procedures are developed by the purchasing department subject to the approval of the administrative head. This relative autonomy allows the department considerable flexibility in the development of systems designed to meet the special needs of the institution. Purchasing is considered to be a support service and, therefore, plays an important part in both operational planning and expansion of facilities or services planning. Purchasing is involved in the acquisition of highly complex medical equipment that is often experimental in nature.

The purchasing department is usually responsible for the procurement of all support materials and equipment, furniture, landscaping equipment and supplies, custodial equipment and supplies, and office equipment, which may also include highly sophisticated computer hardware and software. The department is sometimes also responsible for food service and pharmaceuticals, although in most cases, these items are specified and ordered by the dietary department and the pharmacy. The purchasing systems most often used are the open market quotation and the informal bid procedure.

Considering the nature of the organization, it is not surprising that availability and delivery service is a major factor when selecting vendors. Many of the products and services purchased are vital in life or death situations, and inventory control is especially sensitive to medical requirements. Most medical institutions also have elaborate product and service evaluation systems to ensure that the items meet rigid quality standards. These evaluation or quality control committees also play an important part in developing specifications and standards for new products and equipment since the purchasing department cannot be expected to know all of the medical implications.

Product knowledge is, however, extremely important in the medical field, and it is knowledge that can be gained only through experience. Therefore, it is not unusual for people entering the medical purchasing field to come from some of the technical areas or from complex clerical positions. Although most purchasing officials recommend a degree in business as desirable, the primary emphasis is on product knowledge and a thorough familiarity with medical organizations and their needs. Many of the products are obtained through long-term contracts. Consequently, skill in negotiating is an important asset. As in most other industries, a member of the purchasing staff is involved with every planning and evaluation committee and must be able to work effectively with a cross section of the medical community.

Working Conditions

Working conditions vary. Many newer institutions are spacious and well equipped. In some older institutions, the purchasing department, along with other office staff, is often crammed into whatever space is available, as the size of the staff and the patient load far exceed capacity. The pay scale is average for the industry but below the average of purchasing positions in unrelated industries. Fringe benefits are good, and job stability and security are above average. Opportunities for advancement seem promising as the medical and health fields continue to expand at a rapid rate. The working environment is fast paced because of the number and variety of products and services involved, and the life-or-death element does create a sense of urgency. The need for accuracy and detail is extremely high, as is the need for continuous follow-through. The work group is diverse and interesting because of the variety of professions involved in the day-to-day activities. Most institutions are highly structured and organized with well-defined priorities. Opportunities to use purchasing as a stepping-stone to higher management positions that require a different set of skills are limited. Directors of purchasing are seldom appointed to chief of surgery, for example.

Qualifications

Personnel directors expect candidates for purchasing positions to have strong personal goals and, as one purchasing manager stated, to be mission oriented. They must be emotionally stable with a cheerful outgoing personality, adaptive, innovative, and able to grasp complex concepts quickly. Since confidentiality is often required, they must have good judgment and high ethical standards. They are often the link between a demanding user and the supplier, a situation that requires strong interpersonal relationship and mediation skills.

Also, many purchasing professionals in this field have an exceptionally strong sense of commitment. They are all very much aware of the stakes involved and believe that they are an essential part of a team effort in the delivery of quality health care.

PUBLIC MEDICAL SERVICES

The Nature of the Work

The principal difference between public and private medical service workers is not what they do but how they do it. Since public medical institutions are usually an agency of a state, municipal, or federal government, much of the purchasing is done by some government central purchasing department. However, depending on the special nature of the institution's mission, government control over public institutions, purchasing policies, and procedures differs dramatically. In some cases' the institution is allowed to purchase completely outside the government's system. In other cases, the purchasing function may be shared based on dollar limits or product categories, while in still other instances, the responsibility for purchasing policies and procedures may be vested entirely with the central government. Understanding the nature of the relationship between the government and the institution is extremely important if you are considering a position in this field because the nature of the relationship determines both the experience needed and the personality type best suited for the position.

In situations in which the institution has almost complete autonomy, the determination of policy and procedures is very similar to the private institution, except that the system is probably subject to audit by the government purchasing or general accounting office. This state of relative autonomy really means that the purchasing department may design a purchasing system, including open-market quotations, that will best meet its needs. As long as the system is fair and allows tax-paying suppliers to compete, it will be allowed to continue.

The other extreme is the total control of the purchasing function by the government agency. In this situation, the purchasing department's function, at the institutional level, is primarily a clerical link. Although needs assessment is accomplished at the local level and, in some cases, some of the specifications may be developed locally, the buying process is handled by the government central purchasing department.

Entry Requirements and Qualifications

Entry-level positions vary. Since employment is usually subject to civil service regulations, positions in purchasing are filled according to those policies. If the institution is unionized, then additional requirements may be imposed. You should visit the employment office of the local government and obtain as much information as possible about hiring and promotional practices. Then visit the purchasing office for further information concerning procedures and policies at the local or institutional level. You should be able to determine the degree of autonomy that the purchasing department has in developing its own policies and procedures, which, in turn, will tell you much about job responsibilities and conditions.

This information is so important because, ultimately, working in a bureaucracy demands a certain type of personality. If you function best within a highly structured environment and enjoy following an established routine and rigid guidelines, then working in the public sector might be best for you in terms of job satisfaction.

The desired personality and character traits are basically the same as in the private sector. You must be emotionally stable, not easily frustrated, and have a good sense of organization. You will be required to interact with many departments and, depending on the internal structure, with the centralized purchasing department. Therefore, excellent verbal and written skills are absolutely essential. As stated before, public institutions usually operate according to very rigid purchasing procedures as a matter of public policy. Therefore, attention to detail and strict guidelines is also essential.

Working Conditions

Compensation will probably be higher than the private sector. Fringe benefits are excellent, and civil service employment does offer considerable job security. Working conditions and surrounding facilities vary greatly. Some of the newer institutions have modern equipment and facilities, while many of the older ones show the effects of years of operating on less than adequate budgets.

CHAPTER 11

PURCHASING IN EDUCATION

Purchasing functions in educational institutions fall into two very distinct categories: purchasing in private schools and colleges, which includes private technical and vocational schools; and purchasing in educational institutions in the public sector, which includes municipal or county school districts, state or municipal colleges and universities, and vocational/technical schools.

The product classifications are generally school supplies, textbooks, custodial supplies, food and food service supplies and equipment, classroom and office furniture, maintenance and grounds equipment and supplies, laboratory equipment, and other specialized products and services, depending on the nature of the institution.

Because the environment is centered around education, there is often more emphasis on degrees, even in entry-level positions, than in other industry classifications. Opportunities for those lacking degrees are most often found in the technical areas such as maintenance or food service, where extensive product knowledge is required. The desirability of a degree, however, increases as the level of education increases. For example, a four-year degree is more often required at the college or university level than at the elementary school level.

PRIVATE EDUCATIONAL INSTITUTIONS

The Nature of the Work

In smaller private schools, the purchasing function is usually contained within the business office or administration, and, in fact, it is not unusual for the business manager to also wear the hat of purchasing agent. In these situations, the actual interviewing of salespeople and preparation of orders may be done by department heads and submitted to the business manager for review and approval. As the size of the school increases, purchasing becomes more of a specialized function, and a specific department will be charged with the purchasing responsibility.

The purchasing system most often used is the open-market quotation. The purchasing agent solicits prices by phone or letter and buys the products from whomever has the best price and has historically provided the best quality and service. There are usually no documentation requirements, and the school usually depends on the judgment of the buyer to obtain the best deal. Sometimes, if the order is large, the agent sends out specifications and requests a formal price quotation. This procedure is most often used when purchasing classroom or maintenance equipment.

The work environment is usually very pleasant, and the purchasing agent is able to work quite independently as long as he or she maintains good relations and communications with department heads.

The larger the institution, the more formalized the purchasing function becomes. Buyers are assigned categories of products and services, and more structured systems of purchase requisitions, orders, and receiving reports are maintained. As in smaller schools, the purchasing function is still contained within the administrative or financial services division and is considered to be a support activity.

Purchasing policy and procedures are formulated and established by the head of purchasing and his or her immediate superior, usually the director or vice-president of administrative or financial services. Higher-level educational institutions tend to have very sophisticated systems and operate on the leading edge of purchasing technology, probably because of the availability of information on many subjects from academic departments.

Buyers are responsible for the procurement of a variety of products, ranging from hard goods for the bookstore (which, more often, resembles a department store) to chemicals for the chemistry labs. As in practically every other industry, there must be much interaction between the purchasing department and the using departments. Specifications are developed on a case-by-case basis—in some cases they are developed jointly by the using department, and in other cases the using department originates the specifications and the order.

For buyers, the emphasis is on product knowledge, and since they work in the private sector, they have the authority to commit, subject to the director of purchasing's approval. They can exercise their own judgment regarding the past performance of suppliers.

In addition to the actual buying functions, the director of purchasing is usually in charge of inventory control, central receiving, warehousing, quality control, vendor evaluation, transportation, and travel services. He or she usually serves on several committees, including planning, budget or finance, cost control, policy, facilities, and long-term or strategic planning.

Entry Requirements and Qualifications

What type of person will be successful in the private educational setting? First and foremost, you must be able to communicate verbally and in writing with extremely diverse groups of people, particularly in larger institutions. The composition of the groups that you will be working with include chemists, engineers, philosophers, scientists, mathematicians, social scientists, administrators, and students. You must be patient and even tempered, not easily frustrated, and able to work with both worlds—business and academia. Teamwork is necessary, even critical, when trying to meet the needs of various academic programs.

Working Conditions

What can you expect from a career in purchasing in a private educational setting? First, as noted before, the working environment is pleasant and relatively structured but not regimented. Compensation may be slightly below average; however, any difference may be offset by reduced costs in housing and entertainment. Employment in older or well-established institutions is stable, and the pace is relatively consistent. Fringe benefit packages are usually excellent, and there are numerous activities available at little or no cost.

PUBLIC EDUCATIONAL INSTITUTIONS

The Nature of the Work

Purchasing in public educational institutions is often subject to the same regulations and guidelines that govern state, county, and municipal procurement simply because the source of the operating funds is the same—the taxpayer. The amount of control, however, exercised by the government entity varies considerably, depending upon such factors as the number of schools within a system, the size of the area covered, and the type of governing entity involved. Some elementary and secondary school districts maintain a centralized purchasing system for all schools within the district, while others may be required to buy everything through the government purchasing division. Small isolated rural schools, however, may have the authority to purchase according to their own system.

Large public technical/vocational schools, colleges, and universities often have their own purchasing departments, but policies and procedures are established and monitored by a government entity. For example, a large state university may have the authority to buy those items funded by their own operating budget, but capital items funded by the state general fund must be purchased by the state central purchasing department.

If you are interested in a purchasing career in this area, it is advisable to investigate the overall purchasing system for the institution that you are interested in joining. The overall structure will determine how much autonomy you will have, what the promotional and career opportunities are for the desired location, and the amount of authority you will have to develop your own specifications and buying procedures.

The autonomy issue is important because often the products purchased by a government agency may not be appropriate for use in an educational institution. For example, one major state university had a constant problem with student dissatisfaction because it was required to purchase all of its food products through the state purchasing department. Unfortunately, the food product specifications were designed for use by the state prison system and were not suitable for use in the university kitchens because of a difference in the type of cooking equipment. It took numerous food riots, many letters to the editors of major state newspapers, and some unfavorable television coverage before the university was allowed to develop its own specifications. The university purchasing department, however, took the brunt of the criticism for something that was beyond its control.

In public sector educational institutions, most purchasing systems revolve around the formal bidding procedure. After a needs assessment has determined the products and services required, detailed specifications and bid instructions are prepared and distributed to potential suppliers. Often, invitations to bid are advertised in local newspapers and business journals. In fact, in many states and municipalities, bid advertising is required by local statutes. Usually the bidding documents require that vendors agree to supply the products for a specific period of time at the same price or at a price indexed to some commonly accepted standard. In some cases, bid openings are public and, except in cases in which the purchasing department can demonstrate that the bidder is not qualified, the contract is awarded to the one bidding the lowest price.

The range of products and services is similar to that purchased by private institutions. However, because of the difference in purchasing systems, the public institution requires considerably longer lead time, a fact not always appreciated by academia. Consequently, the need to relate and communicate effectively with all departments is critical.

Working Conditions

In general, working conditions are quite similar to those in private institutions, although the compensation and promotional opportunities are governed by civil service regulations. In many of the larger institutions, particularly in the eastern United States, all levels of employees, even administrators and faculty, are unionized, and therefore many of the internal promotions and privileges are based on seniority. Fringe benefit programs are usually excellent, and civil service is usually highly stable as far as job security is concerned.

Working within a highly structured government environment places some unusual demands on those in purchasing. The sometimes slow-paced tempo of a bureaucracy can be extremely stressful, especially when the various departments are clamoring for their orders. The systems can be so cumbersome that it is difficult to pinpoint responsibility when things go wrong, another situation that can be very frustrating.

Although buyers must have adequate product knowledge, the principal requirement is knowledge of the purchasing system and how to administer that system in the best interests of the taxpayer. Excellent writing skills are essential since the written specification is the only legal communication between the buyer and the seller. An incomplete or poorly written specification may force the institution to accept a product of poor quality or even the wrong product.

So what qualities must you have to work successfully within a public educational institution? You must be able to work within a highly structured organizational framework. You must be detail minded, stress tolerant, a team player, and very even tempered. You must be able to cope with bureaucracy and, as in the private sector, communicate effectively with a diverse group of people who differ widely in terms of their background, culture, and experiences. You must be goal oriented but patient, a problem solver, and be able to project what you could do in several "what if" situations. You must develop the habit of always having a fallback position.

As noted before, the degree of autonomy and authority is a key factor in public education purchasing. Because education involves some very special and unique demands, your ability to meet those demands will depend upon the amount of flexibility and decision making that the system will allow.

CHAPTER 12

PURCHASING IN THE MANUFACTURING INDUSTRY

THE NATURE OF THE WORK

The manufacturing industry is one of the largest employers of purchasing professionals and offers the best opportunity to earn high salaries. Manufacturing is also ninety-nine percent private sector activity and, therefore, uses the entire spectrum of purchasing policies and systems. Companies range in size from small one- or two-person sole proprietorships to giant international corporations employing hundreds of thousands of employees and manufacturing a multitude of products in many locations. The size of the products can range from tiny fasteners to giant airplanes or vehicles. The manufacturing industry was the first to begin to professionalize the purchasing function and recognize it as an essential part of the production process. As in some other industries, the manufacturing industry is gradually replacing the term *purchasing* with *materials management,* recognizing that the responsibilities go far beyond that of just buying the products or services. In the manufacturing context, purchasing or materials management involves planning, scheduling, organizing, and controlling the flow of materials, products, and services in and out of the organization.

Departments contained within purchasing or materials management may include needs assessment and planning, purchasing research, purchasing, receiving and inspection, expediting, traffic or transportation, and disposal/reclamation. In some companies, quality control reports to the head of purchasing.

There are two trends in purchasing technology and procedures that are, at this point, most evident in manufacturing but obviously will be important in other industry classifications. First, the trend toward negotiated long-term supplier contracts, sometimes called win–win agreements, involves the acceptance of a supplier as a quasi-partner in the production process. This type of agreement requires an extraordinary exchange of information, including long-term plans, financial status, and other data that either side would usually consider confidential.

The other trend involves the use of complex tracking systems that identify the location and status of incoming materials or products and compare the data with the original delivery projections. This information is extremely important for companies using just-in-time inventory systems because, if the shipment is behind schedule, the company can either make production adjustments or change to an alternate transportation method. There is little doubt that, as tracking systems become more sophisticated and available, companies in all industries will use them in their specifications and transportation systems. Those of you who are considering a purchasing career are advised to keep up-to-date on both of these trends because they will impact your effectiveness in the future.

It was previously noted that the manufacturing industry uses every type of purchasing system available because the choice of systems is a matter of company policy. There is, however, an exception to that rule. Very often, contracts with the federal government include mandatory bidding requirements and other affirmative action criteria or instructions. Since these requirements are based on federal statutes, they are not negotiable.

The choice of procurement system in nongovernment contracts depends on the product or service being purchased, the size of the purchase, the number of potential suppliers, and the overall condition of the market. If the needed product is of a highly specialized nature, then the buyer's primary concern is finding a supplier or source, not the application of any particular buying method. In fact, several buyers interviewed for this chapter mentioned that finding a sufficient number of potential suppliers to ensure competitive pricing was their most pressing responsibility.

At the higher levels of purchasing management, managers are usually concerned with the development of effective internal systems involving source evaluation, expediting, quote and bid procedures, market forecasting, documenting and tracking charge backs, and transportation. In large companies, these systems are highly structured and organized because of the number of divisions, departments, groups, sections, and projects involved. Because of the complexity of the systems in manufacturing, a few major colleges and universities have developed purchasing, transportation and operations departments within their business schools that offer majors or concentrations at the bachelor's, master's, and, in some cases, doctoral levels. These programs were originally directed at the manufacturing industry, although at this point, the curriculum is expanding to offer a more comprehensive approach to purchasing.

ENTRY REQUIREMENTS AND QUALIFICATIONS

There is no one answer to the question regarding which is more important: product knowledge or expertise in systems. There are so many different types of products and companies that it is impossible to name a general requirement that applies to all situations. It is safe to say that some product knowledge is necessary in all cases, and this knowledge can be gained by experience or by being placed in a formal training program. Increasingly, however, entry-level positions require a bachelor's degree in business, preferably with a major in purchasing (worth two to four thousand dollars more in beginning salary), indicating that basic systems theory is very important in the manufacturing industry.

Entry-level positions exist in practically every department at the assistant or complex clerical level and, in larger companies, in special formal training programs. As far as formal education requirements are concerned, the amount of formal training seems to depend upon the amount of product knowledge required. The positions requiring in-depth technical knowledge value related work experience more than formal education. The amount of product knowledge required also depends on the amount of technical assistance available.

What are the recruiters for the manufacturing industry looking for? They are looking for someone with a diverse background who understands the total picture of production, someone who is inquisitive and outgoing, good with oral and written communications, well organized, not ego-driven, a good listener, a team player with high ethical standards and the ability to relate to a variety of people ranging from engineering to sales, and, as in most other industries, someone who can think in terms of scenarios.

WORKING CONDITIONS

The work environment varies from small, cramped offices to modern spacious suites, not unexpected considering the variety of manufacturing facilities nationwide. The compensation ranges from average to the highest in the purchasing field. College graduates with a major in purchasing may receive from $25,000 to $28,000 per year with excellent benefits. Job stability and security, however, vary. The manufacturing segment of our economy has been involved in a series of adjustments during the past three decades because of advances in technology and increasing foreign competition. Consequently, some segments have disappeared, others have had to diversify, while others have experienced tremendous growth. These up-and-down, in-and-out cycles obviously affect job stability and security. Purchasing, however, does enjoy the reputation of being one of the stable careers in the manufacturing industry. Promotion or advancement opportunities are good to excellent depending upon the segment. You should look at the prospects of any segment of manufacturing that you are considering for employment.

Opportunities for continuing education, seminars, and workshops in the industry are excellent. Large manufacturing companies are usually major players in sponsoring these educational activities and are also strong supporters of professional associations. They actively encourage their employees to obtain professional certifications.

CHAPTER 13

PURCHASING IN THE SERVICE INDUSTRIES

According to the U.S. Department of Labor, the most rapidly growing segment of the United States workforce is the service industries, a category that includes banking, insurance, and other financial and information activities. Since growth also involves a trend toward consolidation and acquisition, numerous companies are emerging as corporate giants that are acquiring other insurance companies and banks that, in themselves, are service systems with many regional branches. One of the tempting fruits to be gained from consolidation and acquisition is the ability to centralize many of the internal functions such as purchasing and general accounting. Contributing to the centralization trend are continual advances in computer technology in information processing industries. Although early proponents of the computer forecasted a paperless society, the reverse of that forecast is currently taking place, as banks and insurance companies now are one of the primary markets for paper products.

As these service industries consolidate, the purchasing function is moving from the branch to the regional headquarters and, in some cases, to the national corporate headquarters, resulting in higher purchasing volumes and increasing specialization. Since, however, consolidation or centralization involves the distribution of products and services to hundreds or even thousands of branch operations, the need for highly sophisticated control and expediting systems is becoming critical.

This continuous growth has transformed the purchasing function from a part-time job for one of the junior loan officers or a senior clerk at a branch location to a full-time position for a highly professional specialist whose purchasing responsibilities involve millions of dollars per year. Now the purchasing department is a vital part of corporate operations, with the head of the department usually occupying a vice-president's position.

THE NATURE OF THE WORK

A buyer in the service industries usually is involved in the procurement of forms and other paper products, office equipment, computer hardware and software, office furnishings, and warehouse equipment. In larger operations, buyers specialize in the purchase of products in two or more categories. A multibranch bank or insurance company uses hundreds or even thousands of different forms, some adapted for computer operations and others to be prepared manually. The design and purchase of these forms require a thorough knowledge of computer-driven communications and internal organization. In service industries, forms are the basis for almost all data and information entered into the company-wide computer system and also serve as a vital reporting link to thousands of clients.

Purchasing office and computer equipment has evolved from the procurement of relatively simple bookkeeping equipment, adding machines, typewriters, and filing system equipment to the purchase or lease of highly complex computer and word processing equipment. Since equipment buyers must work closely with the using departments or branches and the suppliers or contractors, the amount of technical knowledge required has increased tenfold.

Distribution of the thousands of products and equipment to the network of branch offices is usually the primary responsibility of the purchasing department. Some companies operate their own central receiving and distribution centers while others depend on suppliers to distribute the products. Either method, however, requires an intricate scheduling system to ensure that the many branches receive their supplies and products on time and that these items are compatible with the entire network.

ENTRY REQUIREMENTS AND QUALIFICATIONS

Since buyers do become heavily involved in preparing contracts and specifications, they must possess excellent verbal and writing skills and the ability to organize business communications in a logical format. Most buyers in the service industry have had enough general business experience to understand the needs and the complexity of a large business organization.

The consensus among senior buyers and purchasing managers is that the best background for someone entering the service industry is a bachelor's degree in general business rather than finance, principally because the understanding of business systems and organization is so critical. A proficiency in mathematics is necessary, and management and computer training is preferable.

Work experience should be centered around business and customer relations. Some officials favor retail experience because of the emphasis on customer service, and they feel that the branches of the company are their customers. Computer experience is becoming a necessity since all information transfer systems are now computerized. Experience in internal communications is also a plus.

Since many of the products are purchased through relatively long-term purchase agreements, excellent negotiating skills are a must. These skills, however, are often considered to be part of the in-house training process because the contracts are so specialized.

WORKING CONDITIONS

Service industries, especially banking, are goal oriented. Employees are expected to establish work-related objectives, and through review and evaluation processes, their progress towards those objectives is monitored. Supervision, however, is general, and purchasing professionals are usually given considerable freedom in meeting their responsibilities.

The work environment is usually pleasant and professional. The facilities are generally modern and extensive, with heavy emphasis on the proper corporate image. Compensation levels are low average to average in comparison to other industries, but fringe benefits are excellent. The opportunities for advancement are good, especially in organizations that are expanding and acquiring other companies and financial institutions.

High ethical standards are required, and personal appearance must be in line with the overall corporate image. The work environment is somewhat structured, although not to the extent of some other industries.

If you are considering the service industries as a career goal, then you must be detail oriented, disciplined, a team player, and self-directed. Since you will often be working with intangibles, the ability to think out or project how a systems change will affect an entire network is very important.

CHAPTER 14

PURCHASING IN THE GOVERNMENT

THE NATURE OF THE WORK

Billions of dollars a year are spent by federal, state, and local governments, making this industry the largest employer of purchasing professionals. Although the products and services purchased range from paper clips to space vehicles, almost all government agencies have one thing in common: the taxpayer pays the bills. This single fact places some unique limitations or restrictions on the purchasing system that a government purchaser may use. A buyer in the private sector may eliminate a vendor based on undocumented past delivery performance or on the basis of verbal complaints from using departments. A government buyer may also eliminate a vendor for the same reasons, but the action and the reasons must be thoroughly documented, and in many cases, the action is subject to appeal. Government purchasing systems must give everyone a shot at the action, meaning everyone must be given an opportunity to bid on any item or service. The ability to perform must be assumed unless the potential seller cannot meet certain criteria written in the specifications or some related document. These and other requirements place an unusual emphasis on the preparation of the specifications and the other bidding documents which, in term, complicates the entire system.

Although the peculiar requirements of government purchasing have been mentioned in the chapters on education and medical services, it is appropriate to expand on those requirements in this chapter because government purchasing is systems driven. In the private sector, the purchasing manager may adapt the procurement system to the product. He or she may spot-buy an item that is needed immediately, might solicit open-end quotations on standard items, or solicit bids on a major capital purchase. The government buyer, however, is limited in his or her choice of systems by government regulation, statute, or policy and must follow a rigid procedure in all aspects of the purchase.

Federal government procurement programs are separated into two major departments: the general services administration and the military, both obviously purchasing a wide range of products. The military and the national aerospace agency purchase a unique product or service—research and development. They contract the responsibility to develop a product that will perform a specific function. They don't know what it looks like, how it is made, or how it operates. Decisions to buy are made after the prototype is constructed and tested. Negotiating research and development contracts is an extremely complicated process requiring excellent written communications skills and a quick analytical mind. It is also very important to document every step in the negotiating process, which requires a negotiator who is detail oriented and, above all, patient.

When purchasing identifiable products and services, the general services administration and the military, state, and local government agencies primarily use a formal bidding process. Formal bids can be used for one-time purchases or for long-term contracts in which the successful bidder is required to furnish the products and services of one or more agencies over a specific period of time. In most cases, some type of a centralized purchasing organization is used to accomplish two principal purposes: first, to consolidate buying power, and second, to control the system to ensure that it meets the requirements of various statutes and regulations. The systems are highly structured and designed to withstand high visibility. They are also designed to reduce, as much as possible, the opportunity for abuse. Newspapers have been filled with stories of kickbacks and payoffs for decades, and many political machines have lost their power and position as a result of this type of publicity. By placing the purchasing systems in the hands of the civil service, many government entities have sought to insulate their purchasing procedures from political pressure. Although no one will deny that in some cases political pressures still exist, most government agencies are remarkably free of politics.

At the state and municipal levels, purchasing systems are also determined by some type of statute or regulation. In some respects, the purchasing function at this level is subject to even greater scrutiny than at the federal level, principally because the source of the tax dollars is localized. The taxpayer can see what his or her tax dollar is buying. The taxpayer who might ignore abuses at the federal level will fight city hall at the local level.

The system most often used in state and municipal purchasing is the formal bid. Specifications and invitations to bid are highly publicized, and the entire buying procedure is very structured. The range of products and services purchased is enormous, from pens to complicated construction projects. In fact, it is this variety that attracts many purchasing professionals to the area of government procurement. Most states and larger municipalities use a centralized purchasing system, although the various agencies are allowed to buy specialized items below a specified dollar amount.

ENTRY REQUIREMENTS AND QUALIFICATIONS

Entry-level positions are usually subject to civil service regulations. Since expediting jobs are more often found in the manufacturing area, the normal entry in government purchasing is through complex clerical or assistant buyer positions. Most of the training is accomplished though informal on-the-job training programs. Advancement is heavily influenced by seniority and, in some cases, by civil service examinations. Fringe benefits are usually excellent, with length-of-service requirements for retirement less than the private sector. Salary levels are apt to be slightly less than nongovernment entities, and pay raises are usually based on union or employee association negotiations more than merit.

Although product knowledge is important, the most important requirement is the understanding of how government works. As a public employee, you must develop a sensitivity to the public's perceptions. Even though you may be a civil employee and non-political, your actions still reflect on the party in power—a fact that few politicians ignore. Your performance is often judged not only on effectiveness but also upon how it appears to the taxpayer. Following established procedure and providing proper documentation is the only way to succeed with the high visibility usually involved in government employment.

One character trait deserves special attention for government purchasers. The most important attribute that you must possess is personal integrity. In this field you may be subject to two types of pressures. First, those negotiating to sell to the government may promise you monetary rewards if you accept their bid. Also it is not uncommon to be pressured by political figures to buy from their constituents or to buy only from taxpayers in your state or municipality. Restricting potential suppliers to a specific region or political subdivision invites counteractions on the part of neighboring regions. These counteractions or restrictions limit your ability to negotiate the best deals and also restrict markets for your taxpayers. Standing up to these types of pressures is just part of the job in government purchasing.

WORKING CONDITIONS

The working environment varies considerably. You may be working in a new facility with state-of-the-art computers and equipment, or you may be in an old office building stuffed into whatever space is available. Most state and municipal budgets are strained to the breaking point, and adequate working facilities are a low-priority item. If physical working conditions are important to you, you should investigate the facilities before you apply for the position.

Being involved in government purchasing has its advantages and disadvantages. If you are the type of person who feels comfortable in a highly structured environment, if you are very organized and job security is one of your most important work requirements, then government purchasing should be appealing. You should understand however, that purchasing within a bureaucracy can be very frustrating, and the attention to detail required may seem excessive. Those of you who want considerable flexibility and a relatively unstructured environment should probably look to the private sector in your search for a career.

CHAPTER 15

EDUCATIONAL OPPORTUNITIES IN PURCHASING

As discussed earlier, the purchasing function in business and government has evolved over the past four decades from a clerical job to a vital part of the operation of any organization. As a result, educational institutions have responded to the need for formally educated purchasing or materials management professionals by developing special programs at the associate, bachelor, and graduate level. Other institutions now offer courses that relate to materials management in their schools of business and special certificate courses or seminars in their continuing education departments.

Some industries are tending toward requiring bachelor's degrees for entering their training programs, while other industries still rely upon experience as the primary qualification. There is a pattern among industries requiring formal education. Those industries that are systems oriented—they emphasize knowledge of the various purchasing systems and how they relate to the total production process—are more apt to require formal education than those industries that require extensive product knowledge. In the product knowledge-oriented industries, however, degrees or continuing education courses enhance promotional possibilities beyond the buyer level. The bottom line is that in any industry, postsecondary education is necessary if you are to progress to the top of your field.

Typically, schools offering bachelor-level majors in purchasing have a department within the school of business that concentrates on the primary operations and material flow functions within all types of organizations. For example, Arizona State University has a department called Purchasing, Transportation, and Operations (PTO), and students may elect to major in any one of the three areas. Students majoring in purchasing will normally take 50 percent of their course work in general studies, 20 percent in the business core, and the remainder in purchasing/materials management and other related electives. The purchasing core consists of production and operations, purchasing management, traffic and distribution, materials management, purchasing research, and negotiation and purchasing/materials management strategy. Arizona State, as others, offers an MBA track in PTO and a doctoral program in logistics.

As can be seen from the list of colleges and universities offering purchasing-related courses in Appendix A, there is ample opportunity for those presently working in the purchasing field to continue their formal education. Many community and junior colleges also offer courses that are valuable to the purchasing professional. It is important to note that basic management courses are valuable to those who wish to progress into the higher levels of purchasing executives.

The various trade associations, such as the National Association of Purchasing Management or the National Institute of Government Purchasing, also offer numerous seminars for purchasing professionals, many of which can be credited toward a designation as certified purchasing manager (CPM).

CHAPTER 16

THE ROLE OF INTEGRITY IN PURCHASING

As you consider purchasing as a career direction, you should review the recommended character and personality qualifications for each of the industries outlined in this book. You will notice that in each one, integrity and emotional stability have been heavily emphasized. There is a compelling reason that is not always discussed publicly by those of us in purchasing but one that must be dealt with on a day-to-day basis: the awesome responsibility of the control of power.

Purchasing agents and buyers spend money—in some cases, millions of dollars per year. Money in today's society is power, and power is always accompanied by the temptation to misuse or abuse it. The purchasing professional must always remember the source of the money he or she controls and use that control judiciously. The attention of the salespeople and the contractors can sometimes by flattering, but purchasing professionals must remember that this flattery is usually directed at them because of the amount of money they control. The role of the purchasing professional demands exceptional objectivity and a realistic understanding of the difference between the power of the person and the power of the position.

Self-confidence is also often considered an essential personality requirement of effective professionals. Purchasers must not use the power of their position to boost their ego or sense of self-worth. Purchasing professionals must have a realistic sense of who and what they are that exists independently of their position. They must also be able to place in proper perspective the emotional rewards that the wielding of power provides.

There is one other factor that has shattered the careers of some in the purchasing field. In order to better their chances of obtaining business, some, fortunately few, companies offer inducements. These "sweeteners" may be in the form of cash, gifts, or other items of value. Every professional purchasing association and most companies have a purchasing code of ethics that defines the difference between accepting advertising items and accepting items that might be construed as inducements. If you wish to enter the field of purchasing, you must be prepared to accept this code of ethics as a way of life.

The field of purchasing is an exciting, challenging, and rewarding career, but it demands knowledge, skill, dedication, maturity of judgement, and, above all, unquestionable integrity.

UNIVERSITIES AND INSTITUTIONS OFFERING PURCHASING PROGRAMS

Over the past few years the number of universities and institutions offering purchasing programs has almost doubled as academia scrambles to meet the new demand. Although many institutions offer purchasing courses, the list below only notes those who offer degree or certification programs in purchasing or supply management fields. The degrees are usually in business with an emphasis in purchasing, materials management, logistics, or supply management.

KEY

A   Associate's Degree
B   Bachelor's Degree
M   Master's Degree
P   Ph.D. Degree
C   Certificate Program

UNITED STATES

Air Force Institute of Technology
  School of Systems and Logistics
  Wright Patterson Air Force Base, OH
  B, M, C

University of Alabama
Management and Marketing Department
Huntsville, AL
B

Arizona State University
College of Business
Tempe, AZ
B, M, P

University of Arkansas
Department of Marketing and Transportation
Fayettville, AR
B

Bloomfield College
Materials Management
Bloomfield, NJ
B, C

Bowling Green State University
Department of Management
Bowling Green, OH
B, M

Bryant College
Center for Management Development
Smithfield, RI
B, C

University of California (LA)
Department of Business and Management
Los Angeles, CA
B, M, C

University of California (Riverside)
University Extension
Riverside, CA
C

California State University
Department of Management and Finance
Hayward, CA
B, C

California State University (Sacramento)
  Regional and Continuing Education
  Sacramento, CA
  C

Central Piedmont Community College
  Business Administration
  Charlotte, NC
  A

Coastline Community College
  Business and International Studies
  Huntington Beach, CA
  A, C

University of Colorado (Denver)
  Professional Development Program
  Denver, CO
  C

Cuyahoga Community College
  Business Administration Department
  Island Hills, OH
  A, C

De Paul University
  Center for Professional Development
  Chicago, IL
  C

Des Moines Community College
  Management Department
  Des Moines, IA
  C

Duquesne University
  A.J. Palumbo School of Business
  Pittsburgh, PA
  B, M

Ferris State University
  Marketing Department
  Big Rapids, MI
  C

Florida Institute of Technology
  School of Business
  National Capital Region
  Graduate Center
  Alexandria, VA
  B, M

Florida State University
  Marketing Department
  Tallahassee, FL
  B

George Washington University
  School of Business and Public Management
  Washington, DC
  B, M, P

Golden Gate University
  School of Technology and Industry
  San Francisco, CA
  B, M, C

Greenville Technical College
  Business Division
  Greenville, SC
  A, C

Guilford Technical Community College
  Continuing Education
  Jamestown, NC
  A, C

Harper College
  Materials Logistics Management
  Palatine, IL
  A, C

University of Houston (Downtown)
  Department of Business Management and Administrative Services
  Houston, TX
  B

Indiana University (South Bend)
  Department of Continuing Education
  South Bend, IN
  C

University of Indianapolis
  School of Business
  Indianapolis, IN
  A, C

Institute for Management and Technical Development
  Edison, NJ
  C

Lakeshore Technical College
  Business and Marketing
  Cleveland, WI
  A

Lehigh University
  Department of Business
  Bethlehem, PA
  B, M

Lowell University
  Continuing Education Center
  Lowell, MA
  C

Luzerne County Community College
  Business Department
  Nanticoke, PA
  A

University of Massachusetts (Lowell)
  College of Management
  Lowell, MA
  B, C

University of Maryland
  Department of Management and Technology
  College Park, MD
  M

McLennan Community College
  Waco, TX
  A,C

Metropolitan State University
  College of Management
  Minneapolis, MN
  B, M

Metropolitan Community College
  Business Division
  Omaha, NE
  A

Miami State University
  Department of Management
  Oxford, OH
  B

Michigan State University
  Department of Management
  East Lansing, MI
  B, M, P

Montgomery College
  Management Department-
    Germantown Campus
  Rockville, MD
  A, C

New Hampshire College
  Continuing Education Office
  Manchester, NH
  B

University of Nevada (Reno)
  College of Business
  Reno, NV
  B, M

University of New Orleans
  Management Department
  New Orleans, LA
  C

New York University
  School of Continuing Education
  New York, NY
  C

University of North Texas
  Department of Management
  Denton, TX
  B, M, P

Northeastern University
  Business Administration
  Boston, MA
  A, C

Northeast Wisconsin Technical College
  Business and Marketing Department
  Green Bay, WI
  A

University of North Florida
  Management, Marketing, and Logistics
  Jacksonville, FL
  B

Oakton Community College
  Institution for Business and Professional Development
  Des Plaines, IL
  A

Ohio State University
  Department of Management Sciences
  Columbus, OH
  B, M, P

Pennsylvania State University
  Business Logistics Department
  University Park, PA
  B, M, P, C

University of Phoenix
  Center for Distance Education
  Phoenix, AZ
  B, M, C

Portland State University
  Professional Development Center
  Portland, OR
  C

Rock Valley College
  Technology Department
  Rockford, IL
  A, C

Saint Joseph's University
  University College
  Philadelphia, PA
  A, B, C

University of San Diego
  School of Business
  San Diego, CA
  B, M

San Jose State University
  Professional Development Center
  San Jose, CA
  C

Shoreline Community College
  Business Administration Division
  Seattle, WA
  A, C

Sinclair Community College
  Management Department
  Dayton, OH
  A, C

St. Edwards University
  School of Business
  Austin, TX
  M, C

State University of New York (Buffalo)
  Millard Fillmore College
  Buffalo, NY
  B, C

Syracuse University
School of Management
Syracuse, NY
B

Tulsa Junior College
Business Department
Tulsa, OK
A

Virginia Polytechnical Institute and State University
MBA Department
Blacksburg, VA
M, P, C

Webster University
Department of Business
St. Louis, MO
M

Western Michigan University
Haworth College of Business
Kalamazoo, MI
B

Western New England College
Acquisition and Contracting
Woburn, MA
B, M, C

William Rainey Harper College
Business Department
Palatine, IL
A, C

University of Wisconsin (Madison)
Management Institute
Madison, WI

This information was compiled by Tracy Motlok, editorial research assistant for *Purchasing Today Magazine.*

CANADA

Algonquin College
Nepean, Ont.

> 3 year Business Administration; Specialist certificate in Materials and Inventory Management.

B.C. Institute of Technology
B.C.

> Business certificates in Materials Management and Transportation Logistics

Centennial College of Applied Arts
Scarborough, ON

> 3 year degree in Operations Management

Concordia University
Montreal

> Certificate in Purchasing and Inventory Control

Conestoga College
Guelph, ON

> 3 year Business Administration with materials management specialization

McGill University
Montreal

> Certificate in Transportation

Ryerson University
Toronto

> 2 and 3 year Certificates in material management

This information was provided by the Purchasing Management Association of Canada.